MongoDB Administrator's Guide

Over 100 practical recipes to efficiently maintain and administer your MongoDB solution

Cyrus Dasadia

Packt>

BIRMINGHAM - MUMBAI

MongoDB Administrator's Guide

Copyright © 2017 Packt Publishing

All rights reserved. No part of this book may be reproduced, stored in a retrieval system, or transmitted in any form or by any means, without the prior written permission of the publisher, except in the case of brief quotations embedded in critical articles or reviews.

Every effort has been made in the preparation of this book to ensure the accuracy of the information presented. However, the information contained in this book is sold without warranty, either express or implied. Neither the author, nor Packt Publishing, and its dealers and distributors will be held liable for any damages caused or alleged to be caused directly or indirectly by this book.

Packt Publishing has endeavored to provide trademark information about all of the companies and products mentioned in this book by the appropriate use of capitals. However, Packt Publishing cannot guarantee the accuracy of this information.

First published: October 2017

Production reference: 1241017

Published by Packt Publishing Ltd.
Livery Place
35 Livery Street
Birmingham
B3 2PB, UK.
ISBN 978-1-78712-648-0

www.packtpub.com

Credits

Author
Cyrus Dasadia

Reviewers
Nilap Shah
Ruben Oliva Ramos

Commissioning Editor
Amey Varangaonkar

Acquisition Editor
Viraj Madhav

Content Development Editor
Cheryl Dsa

Technical Editor
Dinesh Pawar

Copy Editor
Safis Editing

Project Coordinator
Nidhi Joshi

Proofreader
Safis Editing

Indexer
Aishwarya Gangawane

Graphics
Tania Dutta

Production Coordinator
Shantanu Zagade

About the Author

Cyrus Dasadia has enjoyed tinkering with open source projects since 1996. He has been working as a Linux system administrator and part-time programmer for over a decade. He works at InMobi, where he loves designing tools and platforms. His love for MongoDB blossomed in 2013, when he was amazed by its ease of use and stability. Since then, almost all of his projects have been written with MongoDB as the primary backend. Cyrus is also the creator of an open source alert management system called CitoEngine. His spare time is devoted to trying to reverse-engineer software, playing computer games, or increasing his silliness quotient by watching reruns of Monty Python.

About the Reviewers

Nilap Shah is a lead software consultant with experience across various fields and technologies. He is expert in .NET, Uipath (Robotics) and MongoDB. He is certified MongoDB developer and DBA. He is technical writer as well as technical speaker. He is also providing MongoDB corporate training. Currently, he is working as lead MongoDB consultant and providing solutions with MongoDB technology (DBA and developer projects). His LinkedIn profile can be found at `https://www.linkedin.com/in/nilap-shah-8b6780a/` and can be reachable +91-9537047334 on WhatsApp.

Ruben Oliva Ramos is a computer systems engineer from Tecnologico de Leon Institute, with a master's degree in computer and electronic systems engineering, teleinformatics, and networking specialization from the University of Salle Bajio in Leon, Guanajuato, Mexico. He has more than 5 years of experience in developing web applications to control and monitor devices connected with Arduino and Raspberry Pi using web frameworks and cloud services to build the Internet of Things applications.

He is a mechatronics teacher at the University of Salle Bajio and teaches students of the master's degree in design and engineering of mechatronics systems. Ruben also works at Centro de Bachillerato Tecnologico Industrial 225 in Leon, Guanajuato, Mexico, teaching subjects such as electronics, robotics and control, automation, and microcontrollers at Mechatronics Technician Career; he is a consultant and developer for projects in areas such as monitoring systems and datalogger data using technologies (such as Android, iOS, Windows Phone, HTML5, PHP, CSS, Ajax, JavaScript, Angular, and ASP.NET), databases (such as SQlite, MongoDB, and MySQL), web servers (such as Node.js and IIS), hardware programming (such as Arduino, Raspberry pi, Ethernet Shield, GPS, and GSM/GPRS, ESP8266), and control and monitor systems for data acquisition and programming.

He has authored the book *Internet of Things Programming with JavaScript* and *Advanced Analytics with R and Tableau* by Packt Publishing. He is also involved in monitoring, controlling, and the acquisition of data with Arduino and Visual Basic .NET for Alfaomega.

> *I would like to thank my savior and lord, Jesus Christ, for giving me the strength and courage to pursue this project; my dearest wife, Mayte; our two lovely sons, Ruben and Dario; my dear father, Ruben; my dearest mom, Rosalia; my brother, Juan Tomas; and my sister, Rosalia, whom I love, for all their support while reviewing this book, for allowing me to pursue my dream, and tolerating not being with them after my busy day job.*
> *I'm very grateful to Pack Publishing for giving the opportunity to collaborate as an author and reviewer, to belong to this honest and professional team.*

www.PacktPub.com

For support files and downloads related to your book, please visit www.PacktPub.com. Did you know that Packt offers eBook versions of every book published, with PDF and ePub files available? You can upgrade to the eBook version at www.PacktPub.com and as a print book customer, you are entitled to a discount on the eBook copy. Get in touch with us at service@packtpub.com for more details. At www.PacktPub.com, you can also read a collection of free technical articles, sign up for a range of free newsletters and receive exclusive discounts and offers on Packt books and eBooks.

Mapt

https://www.packtpub.com/mapt

Get the most in-demand software skills with Mapt. Mapt gives you full access to all Packt books and video courses, as well as industry-leading tools to help you plan your personal development and advance your career.

Why subscribe?

- Fully searchable across every book published by Packt
- Copy and paste, print, and bookmark content
- On demand and accessible via a web browser

Customer Feedback

Thanks for purchasing this Packt book. At Packt, quality is at the heart of our editorial process. To help us improve, please leave us an honest review on this book's Amazon page at https://www.amazon.com/dp/178712648X.

If you'd like to join our team of regular reviewers, you can email us at customerreviews@packtpub.com. We award our regular reviewers with free eBooks and videos in exchange for their valuable feedback. Help us be relentless in improving our products!

Table of Contents

Preface — 1

Chapter 1: Installation and Configuration — 7
- **Introduction** — 7
- **Installing and starting MongoDB on Linux** — 8
  - Getting ready — 8
  - How to do it… — 8
  - How it works… — 9
  - There's more… — 10
- **Installing and starting MongoDB on macOS** — 10
  - Getting ready — 10
  - How to do it… — 10
  - How it works… — 12
- **Binding MongoDB process to a specific network interface and port** — 12
  - Getting ready — 12
  - How to do it… — 13
  - How it works… — 14
- **Enabling SSL for MongodDB** — 14
  - Getting ready — 14
  - How to do it.. — 14
  - How it works… — 15
  - There's more… — 16
- **Choosing the right MongoDB storage engine** — 16
  - WiredTiger — 16
  - MMAPv1 — 17
  - The verdict — 17
- **Changing storage engine** — 18
  - Getting ready — 18
  - How to do it… — 18
  - How it works… — 20
- **Separating directories per database** — 20
  - Getting ready — 20
  - How to do it… — 21
  - How it works… — 22
- **Customizing the MongoDB configuration file** — 23

Getting ready	24
How to do it..	24
How it works...	24
There's more...	25
Running MongoDB as a Docker container	25
Getting ready	25
How to do it...	25
How it works...	26
There's more..	27
Chapter 2: Understanding and Managing Indexes	29
Introduction	29
Creating an index	29
Getting ready	30
How it works...	34
There's more...	35
Managing existing indexes	35
Getting ready	36
How to do it...	36
How it works...	39
How to use compound indexes	40
Getting ready	40
How to do it...	40
How it works...	44
There's more...	44
Creating background indexes	45
Getting ready	45
How to do it...	45
How it works...	48
Creating TTL-based indexes	49
Getting ready	49
How to do it...	49
How it works...	50
There's more...	50
Creating a sparse index	51
Getting ready	51
How to do it...	51
How it works...	54
Creating a partial index	54
Getting ready	54

How to do it...	54
How it works...	58
Creating a unique index	59
Getting ready	59
How to do it...	59
How it works...	61

Chapter 3: Performance Tuning — 63

Introduction	63
Configuring disks for better I/O	63
Reading and writing from disks	64
Few considerations while selecting storage devices	66
Measuring disk I/O performance with mongoperf	67
Getting ready	67
How to do it...	67
How it works...	70
Finding slow running queries and operations	72
Getting ready	72
How to do it...	72
How it works...	75
There's more...	76
Storage considerations when using Amazon EC2	77
Figuring out the size of a working set	80
There's more...	82

Chapter 4: High Availability with Replication — 83

Introduction	83
Initializing a new replica set	84
Getting ready	84
How to do it...	85
How it works...	88
Adding a node to the replica set	90
Getting ready	90
How to do it...	90
How it works...	92
Removing a node from the replica set	93
Getting ready	93
How to do it...	93
How it works...	96
Working with an arbiter	97

Getting ready	98
How to do it...	98
How it works...	100
Switching between primary and secondary nodes	**101**
Getting ready	101
How to do it...	101
How it works...	102
Changing replica set configuration	**103**
Getting ready	103
How to do it...	103
How it works..	104
Changing priority to replica set nodes	**105**
Getting ready	105
How to do it...	105
How it works...	106
There's more...	106
Chapter 5: High Scalability with Sharding	**107**
Understanding sharding and its components	**107**
Components of MongoDB sharding infrastructure	108
Config server	108
The mongos query router	108
The shard server	109
Choosing the shard key	109
Setting up and configuring a sharded cluster	**110**
Getting ready	110
How to do it...	110
How it works...	114
Managing chunks	**116**
Getting ready	117
How to do it...	117
How it works...	119
Moving non-sharded collection data from one shard to another	**121**
Getting ready	121
How to do it...	121
How it works...	123
Removing a shard from the cluster	**123**
Getting ready	123
How to do it...	124
How it works...	126

Understanding tag aware sharding – zones	127
Getting ready	127
How to do it...	128
How it works...	129
See also	130

Chapter 6: Managing MongoDB Backups — 131

Introduction	131
Taking backup using mongodump tool	132
Getting ready	132
How to do it...	132
How it works...	134
There's more...	135
Taking backup of a specific mongodb database or collection	135
Getting ready	135
How to do it...	135
How it works...	137
Taking backup of a small subset of documents in a collection	137
Getting ready	137
How to do it...	138
How it works...	138
Using bsondump tool to view mongodump output in human readable form	138
Getting ready	139
How to do it...	139
How it works...	140
Creating a point in time backup of replica sets	141
Getting ready	141
How to do it...	141
How it works...	142
Using the mongoexport tool	143
Getting ready	143
How to do it...	143
How it works...	144
Creating a backup of a sharded cluster	144
Getting ready	144
How to do it...	145
How it works...	145

Chapter 7: Restoring MongoDB from Backups — 147

Introduction	147
Restoring standalone MongoDB using the mongorestore tool	147
Getting ready	148
How to do it...	148
How it works...	149
Restoring specific database or specific collection	149
Getting ready	150
How to do it...	150
How it works...	152
Restoring data from one collection or database to another	153
Getting ready	153
How to do it...	153
How it works...	155
Creating a new MongoDB replica set node using backups	156
Getting ready	156
How to do it...	156
How it works...	158
Restoring a MongoDB sharded cluster from backup	159
Getting ready	159
How to do it...	159
How it works...	160

Chapter 8: Monitoring MongoDB — 161

Introduction	161
Monitoring MongoDB performance with mongostat	162
Getting ready	162
How to do it...	162
How it works...	164
See also	165
Checking replication lag of nodes in a replica set	165
Getting ready	165
How to do it...	166
How it works...	167
Monitoring and killing long running operations on MongoDB	168
Getting ready	168
How to do it...	169
How it works...	171
See also	171
Checking disk I/O usage	171
Getting ready	171

How to do it...	172
How it works...	173
Collecting MongoDB metrics using Diamond and Graphite	174
Getting ready	174
How to do it...	174
How it works...	176
See also	176

Chapter 9: Authentication and Security in MongoDB — 177

Introduction	177
Setting up authentication in MongoDB and creating a superuser account	178
Getting ready	178
How to do it...	178
How it works...	179
Creating normal users and assigning built-in roles	180
Getting ready	180
How to do it...	181
How it works...	182
See also...	184
Creating and assigning custom roles	184
Getting ready	184
How to do it...	184
How it works...	188
Restoring access if you are locked out	189
Getting ready	189
How to do it...	189
How it works...	190
Using key files to authenticate servers in a replica set	191
Getting ready	191
How to do it...	191
How it works...	193
There's more...	194

Chapter 10: Deploying MongoDB in Production — 195

Introduction	195
Configuring MongoDB for a production deployment	195
Getting ready	196
How to do it...	196
Upgrading production MongoDB to a newer version	198

Getting ready	198
How to do it...	198
There's more...	199
Setting up and configuring TLS (SSL)	199
Getting ready	199
How to do it...	200
How it works...	200
There's more...	202
Restricting network access using firewalls	202
Getting ready	202
How to do it...	202
How it works...	203
See also	204
Index	205

Preface

MongoDB is an extremely versatile NoSQL database that offers performance, scalability, and reliability of data. It has slowly become one of the leading NoSQL database systems used for storing extremely large datasets. In addition to this, the fact that it is open source makes it the perfect candidate for any project. From prototyping a minimal viable product to storing millions of complex documents, MongoDB is clearly emerging as the go-to database system.

This book aims to help the reader in operating and managing MongoDB systems. The contents of this book are divided into sections covering all the core aspects of administering MongoDB systems. The primary goal of this book is not to duplicate the MongoDB documentation, but to gently nudge the reader towards topics that are often overlooked when designing MongoDB systems.

What this book covers

Chapter 1, *Installation and Configuration*, covers the basic details of how to install MongoDB, either from the bundled binaries or through the operating system's package managers. It also covers configuration details, as well as how to install MongoDB in a Docker container.

Chapter 2, *Understanding and Managing Indexes*, gives a quick overview of the benefits of indexes, their various types, and how to optimize database responses by choosing the correct indexes.

Chapter 3, *Performance Tuning*, covers various topics that can help optimize the infrastructure to deliver optimal database performance. We discuss disk I/O optimization, measuring slow queries, storage considerations in AWS, and managing working sets.

Chapter 4, *High Availability with Replication*, shows how to achieve high availability using MongoDB replica sets. Topics such as the configuration of replica sets, managing node subscriptions, arbiters, and so on are covered.

Chapter 5, *High Scalability with Sharding*, covers MongoDB's high scalability aspects using shards. The topics covered in this section include setting up a sharded cluster, managing chunks, managing non-sharded data, adding and removing nodes from the cluster, and creating a geographically distributed sharded cluster.

Chapter 6, *Managing MongoDB Backups*, helps the reader understand how to select an optimum backup strategy for their MongoDB setup. It covers how to take backups of standalone systems, replica sets, analyzing backup files, and so on.

Chapter 7, *Restoring MongoDB from Backups*, shows various techniques for restoring systems from previously generated backups. Topics covered include restoring standalone systems, specific databases, the backup of one database to another database, replica sets, and sharded clusters.

Chapter 8, *Monitoring MongoDB*, illustrates various aspects of monitoring the health of a MongoDB setup. This chapter includes recipes for using `mongostat`, monitoring replica set nodes, monitoring long-running operations, checking disk I/O, fetching database metrics, and storing them in a time-series database such as Graphite.

Chapter 9, *Authentication and Security in MongoDB*, looks into various aspects involved in securing a MongoDB infrastructure. Topics covered in this chapter include creating and managing users, implementing role-based access models, implementing SSL/TLS-based transport mechanisms, and so on.

Chapter 10, *Deploying MongoDB in Production*, provides insights into deploying MongoDB in a production environment, upgrading servers to newer versions, using configuration management tools to deploy MongoDB, and using Docker Swarm to set up MongoDB in containers.

What you need for this book

For the most part, this book requires only MongoDB 3.4 or higher. Although most of the operating system commands used throughout the book are for Linux, the semantics is generic and can be replayed on any operating system. It may be useful to have some knowledge of how MongoDB works, but for the most part, all chapters are verbose enough for beginners as well.

Who this book is for

This book is for database administrators or site reliability engineers who are keen on ensuring the stability and scalability of their MongoDB systems. Database administrators who have a basic understanding of the features of MongoDB and want to professionally configure, deploy, and administer a MongoDB database will find this book essential. If you are a MongoDB developer and want to get into MongoDB administration, this book will also help you.

Sections

In this book, you will find several headings that appear frequently (Getting ready, How to do it…, How it works…, There's more…, and See also). To give clear instructions on how to complete a recipe, we use these sections as follows.

Getting ready

This section tells you what to expect in the recipe, and describes how to set up any software or any preliminary settings required for the recipe.

How to do it…

This section contains the steps required to follow the recipe.

How it works…

This section usually consists of a detailed explanation of what happened in the previous section.

There's more…

This section consists of additional information about the recipe in order to make the reader more knowledgeable about the recipe.

See also

This section provides helpful links to other useful information for the recipe.

Conventions

In this book, you will find a number of text styles that distinguish between different kinds of information. Here are some examples of these styles and an explanation of their meaning. Code words in text, database table names, folder names, filenames, file extensions, pathnames, dummy URLs, user input, and Twitter handles are shown as follows: "You can view the available command line parameters by using `--help` or `-h`."

Any command-line input or output is written as follows:

```
ln -s data/mongodb-linux-x86_64-ubuntu1404-3.4.4/ data/mongodb
```

New terms and **important words** are shown in bold.

> Warnings or important notes appear like this.

> Tips and tricks appear like this.

Reader feedback

Feedback from our readers is always welcome. Let us know what you think about this book-what you liked or disliked. Reader feedback is important for us as it helps us develop titles that you will really get the most out of. To send us general feedback, simply e-mail `feedback@packtpub.com`, and mention the book's title in the subject of your message. If there is a topic that you have expertise in and you are interested in either writing or contributing to a book, see our author guide at `www.packtpub.com/authors`.

Customer support

Now that you are the proud owner of a Packt book, we have a number of things to help you to get the most from your purchase.

Downloading the example code

You can download the example code files for this book from your account at `http://www.packtpub.com`. If you purchased this book elsewhere, you can visit `http://www.packtpub.com/support` and register to have the files emailed directly to you. You can download the code files by following these steps:

1. Log in or register to our website using your e-mail address and password.
2. Hover the mouse pointer on the **SUPPORT** tab at the top.
3. Click on **Code Downloads & Errata**.
4. Enter the name of the book in the **Search** box.
5. Select the book for which you're looking to download the code files.
6. Choose from the drop-down menu where you purchased this book from.
7. Click on **Code Download**.

You can also download the code files by clicking on the **Code Files** button on the book's web page at the Packt Publishing website. This page can be accessed by entering the book's name in the **Search** box. Please note that you need to be logged in to your Packt account. Once the file is downloaded, please make sure that you unzip or extract the folder using the latest version of:

- WinRAR / 7-Zip for Windows
- Zipeg / iZip / UnRarX for Mac
- 7-Zip / PeaZip for Linux

The code bundle for the book is also hosted on GitHub at `https://github.com/PacktPublishing/MongoDB-Administrators-Guide`. We also have other code bundles from our rich catalog of books and videos available at `https://github.com/PacktPublishing/`. Check them out!

Errata

Although we have taken every care to ensure the accuracy of our content, mistakes do happen. If you find a mistake in one of our books-maybe a mistake in the text or the code- we would be grateful if you could report this to us. By doing so, you can save other readers from frustration and help us improve subsequent versions of this book. If you find any errata, please report them by visiting http://www.packtpub.com/submit-errata, selecting your book, clicking on the **Errata Submission Form** link, and entering the details of your errata. Once your errata are verified, your submission will be accepted and the errata will be uploaded to our website or added to any list of existing errata under the Errata section of that title. To view the previously submitted errata, go to https://www.packtpub.com/books/content/support and enter the name of the book in the search field. The required information will appear under the **Errata** section.

Piracy

Piracy of copyrighted material on the Internet is an ongoing problem across all media. At Packt, we take the protection of our copyright and licenses very seriously. If you come across any illegal copies of our works in any form on the Internet, please provide us with the location address or website name immediately so that we can pursue a remedy. Please contact us at copyright@packtpub.com with a link to the suspected pirated material. We appreciate your help in protecting our authors and our ability to bring you valuable content.

Questions

If you have a problem with any aspect of this book, you can contact us at questions@packtpub.com, and we will do our best to address the problem.

1
Installation and Configuration

In this chapter, we will cover the following recipes:

- Installing and starting MongoDB on Linux
- Installing and starting MongoDB on macOS
- Binding MongoDB process to a specific network interface and port
- Enabling SSL for MongoDB
- Choosing the right MongoDB storage engine
- Changing storage engine
- Separating directories per database
- Customizing the MongoDB configuration file
- Running MongoDB as a Docker container

Introduction

In this chapter, we will look at how to install a standalone MongoDB server. We will also look at how to perform some useful customization to the default configuration of a MongoDB server. Lastly, we will run a MongoDB server inside a Docker container.

> MongoDB 3.4 was the latest stable release available while writing this book. All recipes in this and the subsequent chapters assume you are using MongoDB 3.4 or higher.

Installing and starting MongoDB on Linux

Getting ready

You will need a machine running Ubuntu 14.04 or higher, although in theory any Red Hat or Debian-based Linux distribution should be fine. You will also need to download the latest stable binary tarball from `https://www.mongodb.com/download-center`.

How to do it...

1. Create a directory `/data` and untar your downloaded file into this directory so that you now have a `/data/mongodb-linux-x86_64-ubuntu1404-3.4.4` directory. All of MongoDB's core binaries are available in the `/data/mongodb-linux-x86_64-ubuntu1404-3.4.4/bin` directory.

2. Create a symbolic link to the versioned file directory for a simpler naming convention and also allowing us to use a generic directory name (for example, in scripts):

   ```
   ln -s /data/mongodb-linux-x86_64-ubuntu1404-3.4.4/ /data/mongodb
   ```

3. Create a directory for the database:

   ```
   mkdir /data/db
   ```

4. Start the MongoDB server:

   ```
   /data/mongodb/bin/mongod --dbpath /data/db
   ```

5. You should see output like this:

   ```
   2017-05-14T10:07:15.247+0000 I CONTROL  [initandlisten] MongoDB starting : pid=3298 port=27017 dbpath=/data/db 64-bit host=vagrant-ubuntu-trusty-64
    2017-05-14T10:07:15.247+0000 I CONTROL  [initandlisten] db version v3.4.4
    2017-05-14T10:07:15.248+0000 I CONTROL  [initandlisten] git version: 888390515874a9debd1b6c5d36559ca86b44babd
    2017-05-14T10:07:15.248+0000 I CONTROL  [initandlisten] OpenSSL version: OpenSSL 1.0.1f 6 Jan 2014
    2017-05-14T10:07:15.248+0000 I CONTROL  [initandlisten] allocator: tcmalloc
   ```

```
  2017-05-14T10:07:15.249+0000 I CONTROL   [initandlisten] modules:
none
  2017-05-14T10:07:15.249+0000 I CONTROL   [initandlisten] build
environment:
  2017-05-14T10:07:15.249+0000 I CONTROL   [initandlisten]
distmod: ubuntu1404
  2017-05-14T10:07:15.249+0000 I CONTROL   [initandlisten]
distarch: x86_64
  2017-05-14T10:07:15.250+0000 I CONTROL   [initandlisten]
target_arch: x86_64
  2017-05-14T10:07:15.250+0000 I CONTROL   [initandlisten] options: {
storage: { dbPath: "/data/db" } }
  < -- snip -- >
  2017-05-14T10:07:15.313+0000 I COMMAND   [initandlisten] setting
featureCompatibilityVersion to 3.4
  2017-05-14T10:07:15.313+0000 I NETWORK   [thread1] waiting for
connections on port 27017
```

6. You can stop the server by pressing *Ctrl + C*.
7. Additionally, for convenience, we can edit the system's PATH variable to include the mongodb binaries directory. This allows us to invoke the mongodb binaries without having to type the entire path. For example, to execute the mongo client, instead of having to type /data/mongodb/bin/mongo every time, we can simply type mongo. This can be done by appending your ~/.bashrc or ~/.zshrc files for bash and zsh respectively, with the following lines:

```
PATH=/data/mongodb/bin:${PATH}
export PATH
```

How it works...

We downloaded a precompiled binary package and started the mongod server using the most basic command line parameter --dbpath so that it uses a customized directory, /data/db for storing databases. As you might have noticed, the MongoDB server by default, starts listening on TCP port 27017 on all interfaces.

Installation and Configuration

There's more...

The mongod binary has a lot of interesting options. You can view the available command line parameters by using `--help` or `-h`. Alternatively, you can also find a detailed reference of available options, at https://docs.mongodb.com/master/reference/program/mongod/.

Just like most mature community projects, MongoDB also provides packages for formats supported by Debian/Ubuntu and Red Hat/CentOS package managers. There is extensive documentation on how to configure your operating system's package manager to automatically download the MongoDB package and install it. For more information on how to do so, see: https://docs.mongodb.com/master/administration/install-on-linux/.

Installing and starting MongoDB on macOS

Similar to the previous recipe, *Installing and starting MongoDB on Linux*, we will see how to set up MongoDB on a macOS operating system.

Getting ready

MongoDB supports macOS 10.7 (Lion) or higher, so ensure that your operating system is upgraded. Download the binary files the latest stable binary tarball from https://www.mongodb.com/download-center.

How to do it...

1. In this recipe, we will be installing MongoDB in the user's home directory. Create a directory `~/data/` and extract the TAR file in this directory:

   ```
   tar xvf mongodb-osx-x86_64-3.4.4.tgz
   ```

   All of MongoDB's core binaries are available in the `~/data/mongodb-osx-x86_64-3.4.4/bin` directory.

Installation and Configuration

2. Create a symbolic link to the versioned file directory for simpler naming conventions and also allowing us to use a generic directory name (for example, in scripts):

   ```
   cd ~/data/
   ln -s mongodb-osx-x86_64-3.4.4 mongodb
   ```

3. Create a directory for the database:

   ```
   mkdir ~/data/db
   ```

4. Start the MongoDB server:

   ```
   ~/data/mongodb/bin/mongod --dbpath ~/data/db
   ```

5. You should see output like this:

   ```
   2017-05-21T15:21:20.662+0530 I CONTROL  [initandlisten] MongoDB starting : pid=960 port=27017 dbpath=/Users/cyrus.dasadia/data/db 64-bit host=foo
    2017-05-21T15:21:20.662+0530 I CONTROL  [initandlisten] db version v3.4.4
    2017-05-21T15:21:20.662+0530 I CONTROL  [initandlisten] git version: 888390515874a9debd1b6c5d36559ca86b44babd
    2017-05-21T15:21:20.662+0530 I CONTROL  [initandlisten] allocator: system
    2017-05-21T15:21:20.662+0530 I CONTROL  [initandlisten] modules: none
    2017-05-21T15:21:20.662+0530 I CONTROL  [initandlisten] build environment:
    2017-05-21T15:21:20.662+0530 I CONTROL  [initandlisten] distarch: x86_64
    2017-05-21T15:21:20.662+0530 I CONTROL  [initandlisten] target_arch: x86_64
    2017-05-21T15:21:20.662+0530 I CONTROL  [initandlisten] options: { storage: { dbPath: "/Users/cyrus.dasadia/data/db" } }
    <<--- snip -- >>
    2017-05-21T15:21:21.492+0530 I NETWORK  [thread1] waiting for connections on port 27017
   ```

6. You can press *Ctrl + C* to stop the server.

7. Additionally, for convenience, we can edit the system's `PATH` variable to include the MongoDB binaries directory. This allows us invoke the MongoDB binaries without having to type the entire path. For example, to execute the mongo client, instead of having to type `~/mongodb/bin/mongo` every time we can simply type `mongo`. This can be done by appending your `~/.bashrc` or `~/.zshrc` files for `bash` and `zsh` respectively, with the following lines:

```
PATH=~/data/mongodb/bin:${PATH}
export PATH
```

How it works...

Similar to our first recipe, we downloaded a precompiled binary package and started the MongoDB server using the most basic command line parameter `--dbpath` such that it uses a customized directory `~/data/db` for storing databases. As you might have noticed, MongoDB server by default, starts listening on TCP `27017` on all interfaces. We also saw how to add the MongoDB binary directory's path to our system's `PATH` variable for a more convenient way to access the MongoDB binaries.

Binding MongoDB process to a specific network interface and port

As you might have observed, after starting the MongoDB server, the mongod process binds to all interfaces which may not be suitable for all use cases. For example, if you are using MongoDB for development or you are running a single node instance on the same server as your application, you probably do not wish to expose MongoDB to the entire network. You might also have a server with multiple network interfaces and may wish to have MongoDB server listen to a specific network interface. In this recipe, we will see how to start MongoDB on a specific interface and port.

Getting ready

Make sure you have MongoDB installed on your system as shown in the previous recipes.

How to do it...

1. Find your system's network interfaces and corresponding IP address(es) using the `ifconfig` command. For example, let's assume your system's IP address is `192.168.1.112`.
2. Start the mongod daemon without any special flags:

    ```
    mongod --dbpath /data/db
    ```

    This starts the mongod daemon which binds to all network interfaces on port `27017`.

3. In a separate Terminal, connect to your MongoDB server on this IP:

    ```
    mongo 192.168.1.112:27017
    ```

    You should see a MongoDB shell.

4. Now stop the previously running mongod daemon (press *Ctrl + C* in the Terminal) and start the daemon to listen to your loopback interface:

    ```
    mongod --dbpath /data/db --bind_ip 127.0.0.1
    ```

5. In a separate Terminal, connect to your MongoDB server on this IP:

    ```
    mongo 192.168.1.112:27017
    ```

6. This time the mongo client will exit with a `connect failed` message. Let's connect to your loopback IP and it should work:

    ```
    mongo 127.0.0.1:27017
    ```

7. Stop the mongod daemon (press *Ctrl + C* in the Terminal) and let's start the daemon such that it binds to a different port as well:

    ```
    mongod --dbpath /data/db --bind_ip 127.0.0.1 --port 27000
    ```

8. In a separate Terminal, connect to your MongoDB server on this IP:

    ```
    mongo 127.0.0.1:27000
    ```

9. You should be connected to the server and see the mongo shell.

Installation and Configuration

How it works...

By default, the mongod daemon binds to all interfaces on TCP port 27017. By passing the IP address with the `--bind_ip` parameter, we instructed mongod daemon to listen only on this socket. Next we passed the `--port` parameter along with `--bind_ip` to instruct the mongod daemon to listen to a particular port and IP. Using a non-standard port is a common practice when one wishes to run multiple instances of mongod daemon (along with a different `--dbpath`) or wish to add a little touch security by obscurity. Either way, we will be using this practice in our later recipes to test shards and replica sets setups running on a single server.

Enabling SSL for MongodDB

By default, connections to MongoDB server are not encrypted. If one were to intercept this traffic, almost all the data transferred between the client and the server is visible as clear text. If you are curious, I would encourage you to use `tcpdump` or `wireshark` to capture packets between a mongod daemon and the client. As a result, it is highly advisable to make sure that you encrypt all connections to your mongod set by enabling **Transport Layer Security** (**TLS**) also commonly known as SSL.

Getting ready

Make sure you have MongoDB installed on your system as shown in the previous recipes.

> The default MongoDB binaries for OS X are not compiled with SSL, you may need to manually recompile the source code or use Homebrew:
> `brew install mongodb --with-openssl`.

How to do it..

1. First, let us generate a self-signed certificate using OpenSSL, in the `/data` directory:

    ```
    openssl req -x509 -newkey rsa:4096 -nodes -keyout mongo-secure.key -out mongo-secure.crt -days 365
    ```

[14]

Installation and Configuration

2. Combine the key and certificate into a single `.pem` file:

   ```
   cat mongo-secure.key mongo-secure.crt > mongo-secure.pem
   ```

3. Start the mongod daemon, with SSL enabled and listening on the default socket that is, localhost `27017`:

   ```
   mongod --dbpath /data/db --sslMode requireSSL --sslPEMKeyFile /data/mongo-secure.pem
   ```

4. In another window, connect to this server using a mongo client:

   ```
   mongo localhost:27017
   ```

5. You should see a `connect failed` error on the client Terminal. Switch to the server's console window and you should see a log message indicating that the connection was rejected, something like this:

   ```
   2017-05-13T16:51:08.031+0000 I NETWORK  [thread1] connection accepted from 192.168.200.200:43441 #4 (1 connection now open)
   2017-05-13T16:51:08.032+0000 I -        [conn4] AssertionException handling request, closing client connection: 17189 The server is configured to only allow SSL connections
   2017-05-13T16:51:08.032+0000 I -        [conn4] end connection 192.168.200.200:43441 (1 connection now open)
   ```

6. Now, switch back to the other console window and connect to the server again but this time using SSL:

   ```
   mongo --ssl --sslAllowInvalidCertificates
   ```

7. You should be connected to the server and see the mongo shell.

How it works...

In step 1, we created a self-signed certificate to get us started with SSL enabled connections. One could very well use a certificate signed by a valid **Certificate Authority** (**CA**), but for test purposes we are good with a self-signed certificate. In all honesty, if connection security is all you need, a self-signed certificate can also be used in a production environment as long as you keep the keys secure. You might as well take it a step forward by creating your own CA certificate and use it to sign your certificates.

In step 2, we concatenate the key and the certificate file. Next, in step 3, we start the mongod daemon with `--sslMode requireSSL` followed by providing the path to the concatenated `.pem` file. At this point, we have a standalone MongoDB server listening to the default port `27017`, ready to accept only SSL based clients.

Next, we attempt to connect to the mongod server using the default non-SSL mode, which is immediately rejected by the sever. Finally, in step 5 we explicitly make an SSL connection by providing the `--ssl` parameter followed by `--sslAllowInvalidCertificates`. The latter parameter is used because we are using a self-signed certificate on the server. If we were using an certificate signed by a authorized CA or even a self-signed CA, we could very well use the `--sslCAFile` to provide the CA certificate.

There's more…

MongoDB also supports *X.509* certificate-based authentication as an option to username and passwords. We will cover this topic in `Chapter 9`, *Authentication and Security in MongoDB*.

Choosing the right MongoDB storage engine

Starting with MongoDB Version 3.0, a new storage engine named WiredTiger was available and very soon it became the default storage engine in version 3.2. Up until then, MMAPv1 was used as the default storage engine. I will give you a brief rundown on the main features of both storage engines and hopefully it should give you enough to decide which one suits your application's requirements.

WiredTiger

WiredTiger provides the ability, for multiple clients, to perform write operations on the same collection. This is achieved by providing document-level concurrency such that during a given write operation, the database only locks a given document in the collection as against its predecessors, which would lock the entire collection. This drastically improves performance for write heavy applications. Additionally, WiredTiger provides compression of data for indexes and collections. The current compression algorithms used by WiredTiger are Google's Snappy and zLib. Although disabling compression is possible, one should not immediately jump this gun unless it is truly load-tested while planning your storage strategy.

WiredTiger uses **Multi-Version Concurrency Control** (**MVCC**) that allows asserting point-in-time snapshots of transactions. These finalized snapshots are written to disk which helps create checkpoints in the database. These checkpoints eventually help determine the last good state of data files and helps in recovery of data during abnormal shutdowns. Additionally, journaling is also supported with WiredTiger where write-ahead transaction logs are maintained. The combination of journaling and checkpoints increases the chance of data recovery during failures. WiredTiger uses internal caching as well as filesystem cache to provide faster responses on queries. With high concurrency in mind, the architecture of WiredTiger is such that it better utilizes multi-core systems.

MMAPv1

MMAPv1 is quite mature and has proven to be quite stable over the years. One of the storage allocation strategies used with this engine is the power of two allocation strategy. This primarily involves storing double the amount of document space (in power of twos) such that in-place updates of documents become highly likely without having to move the documents during updates. Another storage strategy used with this engine is fixed sizing. In this, the documents are padded (for example, with zeros) such that maximum data allocation for each document is attained. This strategy is usually followed by applications that have fewer updates.

Consistency in MMAPv1 is achieved by journaling, where writes are written to a private view in memory which are written to the on-disk journal. Upon which the changes are then written to a shared view that is the data files. There is no support for data compression with MMAPv1. Lastly, MMAPv1 heavily relies on page caches and hence uses up available memory to retain the working dataset in cache thus providing good performance. Although, MongoDB does yield (free up) memory, used for cache, if another process demands it. Some production deployments avoid enabling swap space to ensure these caches are not written to disk which may deteriorate performance.

The verdict

So which storage engine should you choose? Well, with the above mentioned points, I personally feel that you should go with WiredTiger as the document level concurrency itself is a good marker for attaining better performance. However, as all engineering decisions go, one should definitely not shy away from performing appropriate load testing of the application across both storage engines.

Installation and Configuration

> The enterprise MongoDB version also provides in-memory storage engine and supports encryption at rest. These are good features to have depending on your application's requirements.

Changing storage engine

In this recipe, we will look at how to migrate existing data onto a new storage engine. MongoDB does not allow on the fly (live) migrations, so we will have to do it the hard way.

Getting ready

Ensure you have a MongoDB database installation ready.

How to do it...

1. Start the mongod daemon to explicitly use MMAPv1 storage engine:

   ```
   /data/mongodb/bin/mongod --dbpath /data/db --storageEngine mmapv1
   ```

2. Start the mongo client and you should be presented with the MongoDB shell. Execute the following commands in the shell:

   ```
   > var status = db.serverStatus()
   > status['storageEngine']
   {
      "name" : "mmapv1",
      "supportsCommittedReads" : false,
      "readOnly" : false,
      "persistent" : true
   }
   ```

Installation and Configuration

3. Now let's add some random data into it. Run the following JavaScript code to insert 100 documents with random data:

   ```
   > use mydb
   > for(var x=0; x<100; x++){
     db.mycol.insert({
         age:(Math.round(Math.random()*100)%20)
         })
     }
   > db.mycol.count()
   100
   ```

4. Exit the shell and perform a full backup using `mongodump` command:

   ```
   mkdir /data/backup
   mongodump -o /data/backup --host localhost:27017
   ```

5. Now shutdown the mongod process.
6. Create a new data directory for the migration and start the mongod daemon with a new storage engine:

   ```
   mkdir /data/newdb
   /data/mongodb/bin/mongod --dbpath /data/newdb --storageEngine wiredTiger
   ```

7. Let's restore the previous backup to this new instance:

   ```
   mongorestore /data/backup/
   ```

8. Start the mongo shell and check your data:

   ```
   > var status = db.serverStatus()
   > status['storageEngine']
   {
       "name" : "wiredTiger",
       "supportsCommittedReads" : true,
       "readOnly" : false,
       "persistent" : true
   }
   > use mydb
   switched to db mydb
   > db.mycol.count()
   100
   ```

Installation and Configuration

How it works...

As WiredTiger is the default storage engine for MongoDB 3.2, for this exercise, we explicitly started a MongoDB instance with MMAPv1 storage engine in step 1. In step 2, we stored the `db.serverStatus()` command's output in a temporary variable to inspect the output of the server's `storageEngine` key. This helps us see which storage engine our MongoDB instance is running on. In step 3, we switched to database `mydb` and ran a simple JavaScript function to add 100 documents to a collection called `mycol`. Next, in step 4, we created a backup directory `/data/backup` which is passed as a parameter to `mongodump` utility. We will discuss more about the `mongodump` utility in *Chapter 6, Managing MongoDB Backups*.

Once we shutdown the mongod instance, in step 5, we are now ready to start a new instance of MongoDB but this time with WiredTiger storage engine. We follow the basic practice of covering for failure and instead of removing `/data/db`, we create a new path for this instance (*#AlwaysHaveABackupPlan*). Our new MongoDB instance is empty, so in step 7 we import the aforementioned backup into the database using the `mongorestore` utility. As the new MongoDB instance is running WiredTiger storage engine, our backup (which is essentially BSON data) is restored and saved on disk using this storage engine. Lastly, in step 8, we simply inspect the `storageEngine` key on the `db.serverStatus()` output and confirm that we are indeed using WiredTiger.

As you can see, this is an overly simplistic example of how to convert MongoDB data from one storage engine format to another. One has to keep in mind that this operation will take a significant amount of time depending on the size of data. However, application downtime can be averted if we were to use a replica set. More on this later.

Separating directories per database

In this recipe we will be looking at how to optimize on disk I/O by separating databases in different directories.

Getting ready

Ensure you have a MongoDB database installation ready.

How to do it...

1. Start mongod daemon with no special parameters:

   ```
   /data/mongodb/bin/mongod --dbpath /data/db
   ```

2. Connect to mongo shell, create a test db and insert a sample document:

   ```
   mongo localhost:27017
   > use mydb
   > db.mycol.insert({foo:1})
   ```

3. Inspect the /data/db directory structure, it should look something like this:

   ```
   ls /data/db
   total 244
   drwxr-xr-x  4 root root  4096 May 21 08:45 .
   drwxr-xr-x 10 root root  4096 May 21 08:42 ..
   -rw-r--r--  1 root root 16384 May 21 08:43 collection-0-6262937682035576611.wt
   -rw-r--r--  1 root root 16384 May 21 08:43 collection-2-6262937682035576611.wt
   -rw-r--r--  1 root root 16384 May 21 08:43 collection-5-6262937682035576611.wt
   drwxr-xr-x  2 root root  4096 May 21 08:45 diagnostic.data
   -rw-r--r--  1 root root 16384 May 21 08:43 index-1-6262937682035576611.wt
   -rw-r--r--  1 root root 16384 May 21 08:43 index-3-6262937682035576611.wt
   -rw-r--r--  1 root root 16384 May 21 08:43 index-4-6262937682035576611.wt
   -rw-r--r--  1 root root 16384 May 21 08:43 index-6-6262937682035576611.wt
   drwxr-xr-x  2 root root  4096 May 21 08:42 journal
   -rw-r--r--  1 root root 16384 May 21 08:43 _mdb_catalog.wt
   -rw-r--r--  1 root root     6 May 21 08:42 mongod.lock
   -rw-r--r--  1 root root 16384 May 21 08:44 sizeStorer.wt
   -rw-r--r--  1 root root    95 May 21 08:42 storage.bson
   -rw-r--r--  1 root root    49 May 21 08:42 WiredTiger
   -rw-r--r--  1 root root  4096 May 21 08:42 WiredTigerLAS.wt
   -rw-r--r--  1 root root    21 May 21 08:42 WiredTiger.lock
   -rw-r--r--  1 root root   994 May 21 08:45 WiredTiger.turtle
   -rw-r--r--  1 root root 61440 May 21 08:45 WiredTiger.wt
   ```

4. Shutdown the previous mongod instance.

Installation and Configuration

5. Create a new `db` path and start mongod with `--directoryperdb` option:

   ```
   mkdir /data/newdb
   /data/mongodb/bin/mongod --dbpath /data/newdb --directoryperdb
   ```

6. Connect to the mongo shell, create a test `db`, and insert a sample document:

   ```
   mongo localhost:27017
   > use mydb
   > db.mycol.insert({bar:1})
   ```

7. Inspect the `/data/newdb` directory structure, it should look something like this:

   ```
   ls /data/newdb
   total 108
   drwxr-xr-x  7 root root  4096 May 21 08:42 .
   drwxr-xr-x 10 root root  4096 May 21 08:42 ..
   drwxr-xr-x  2 root root  4096 May 21 08:41 admin
   drwxr-xr-x  2 root root  4096 May 21 08:42 diagnostic.data
   drwxr-xr-x  2 root root  4096 May 21 08:41 journal
   drwxr-xr-x  2 root root  4096 May 21 08:41 local
   -rw-r--r--  1 root root 16384 May 21 08:42 _mdb_catalog.wt
   -rw-r--r--  1 root root     0 May 21 08:42 mongod.lock
   drwxr-xr-x  2 root root  4096 May 21 08:41 mydb
   -rw-r--r--  1 root root 16384 May 21 08:42 sizeStorer.wt
   -rw-r--r--  1 root root    95 May 21 08:41 storage.bson
   -rw-r--r--  1 root root    49 May 21 08:41 WiredTiger
   -rw-r--r--  1 root root  4096 May 21 08:42 WiredTigerLAS.wt
   -rw-r--r--  1 root root    21 May 21 08:41 WiredTiger.lock
   -rw-r--r--  1 root root   986 May 21 08:42 WiredTiger.turtle
   -rw-r--r--  1 root root 28672 May 21 08:42 WiredTiger.wt
   ```

How it works...

We start by running a mongod instance with no special parameters except for `--dbpath`. In step 2, we create a new database `mydb` and insert a document in the collection `mycol`, using the mongo shell. By doing this, the data files for this new `db` are created and can be seen by inspecting the directory structure of our main database path `/data/db`. In that, among other files, you can see that database files begin with `collection-<number>` and its relevant index file begins with `index-<number>`. As we guessed, all databases and their relevant files are within the same directory as our `db` path.

Installation and Configuration

If you are curious and wish to find the correlation between the files and the `db`, then run the following commands in mongo shell:

```
> use mydb
> var curiosity = db.mycol.stats()
> curiosity['wiredTiger']['uri']
statistics:table:collection-5-626293768203557661
```

The last part of this string that is, `collection-5-626293768203557661` corresponds to the file in our `/data/db` path.

Moving on, in steps 4 and step 5, we stop the previous mongod instance, create a new path for our data files and start a new mongod instance but this time with the `--directoryperdb` parameter. As before, in step 6 we insert some random data in the `mycol` collection of a new database called `mydb`. In step 7, we look at the directory listing of our data path and we can see that there is a subdirectory in the data path which, as you guessed, matches our database name `mydb`. If you look inside this directory that is, `/data/newdb/mydb`, you should see a collection and an index file.

So one might ask, why go through all this trouble for having separate directories for databases? Well, in certain application scenarios, if your database workloads are significantly high, you should consider storing the database on a separate disk/volume. Ideally, this should be a physically separate disk or a RAID volume created using separate physical disks. This ensures the separation of disk I/O from other operations including MongoDB journals. Additionally, this also helps you separate your fault domains. One thing you should keep in mind is that journals are stored separately, that is, outside the database's directory. So, using separate disks for databases allows the journals to not content for same disk I/O path.

Customizing the MongoDB configuration file

In all the previous recipes of this chapter, we have passed command line flags to the mongod daemon. In this recipe, we will look at how to use the config file as an alternative to passing command line flags.

Installation and Configuration

Getting ready

Nothing special, just make sure you have a MongoDB database installation ready.

How to do it..

1. Start your favorite text editor and add the following in a file called `mongod.conf`:

   ```
   storage:
     dbPath: /data/db
     engine: wiredTiger
     directoryPerDB: true
   net:
     port: 27000
     bindIp: 127.0.0.1
     ssl:
       mode: requireSSL
       PEMKeyFile: /data/mongo-secure.pem
   ```

2. Start your mongod instance:

   ```
   mongodb/bin/mongod --config /data/mongod.conf
   ```

How it works...

MongoDB allows passing command line parameters to mongod using a YAML file. In step 1, we are creating a config file called `mongod.conf`. We add all the previously used command line parameters from this chapter, into this config file in YAML format. A quick look at the file's content should make it clear that the parameters are divided into sections and relevant subsections. Next, in step 2, we start the mongod instance, but this time with just one parameter `--config` followed by the path of our config file.

As we saw in earlier recipes, although passing configuration parameters seems normal, it is highly advisable that one should use configuration files instead. Having all parameters in a single configuration file not only makes it easier in terms of viewing the parameters but also helps us programmatically (YAML FTW!) inspect and manage the values of these variables. This simplifies operations and reduces the chance of errors.

There's more...

Do have a look at other parameters available in the configuration file `https://docs.mongodb.com/manual/reference/configuration-options/`.

Running MongoDB as a Docker container

In this recipe, we will look at how to run MongoDB as a Docker container. I will assume that you are familiar with the bare minimum understanding of how Docker works. If you are not, have a look at `https://www.docker.com/what-container`. It should help you get acquainted with Docker's concepts.

Getting ready

Make sure you have Docker installed on your system. If you are using Linux, then it is highly advisable to use kernel version 3.16 or higher.

How to do it...

1. Download the latest MongoDB Docker image:

    `docker pull mongo:3.4.4`

2. Check that the image exists:

    `docker images`

3. Start a container:

    `docker run -d -v /data/db:/data/db --name mymongo mongo:3.4.4`

4. Check if the container is running successfully:

    `docker ps`

5. Let's connect to our mongo server using the mongo client from the container:

   ```
   docker exec -it mymongo mongo
   ```

6. Stop the mongo instance and with host mode networking:

   ```
   docker run -d -v /data/db:/data/db --name mymongo --net=host mongo:3.4.4 --bind_ip 127.0.0.1 --port 27000
   ```

7. Connect to the new instance using mongo shell:

```
docker exec -it mymongo mongo localhost:27000
```

How it works...

In step 1, we fetched the official MongoDB image, from Docker's public repository. You can view it at `https://hub.docker.com/_/mongo/`. While fetching the image we explicitly mentioned the version that is, `mongo:3.4.4.`. Although mentioning the version (also known as Docker image tag) is optional, it is highly advisable that when you download any application images via Docker, always fetch them with the relevant tag. Otherwise, you might end up fetching the latest tag and as they change often, you would end up running different versions of you applications.

Next, in step 2, we run the `docker images` command which shows us a list of images available on the server, in our case it should show you the MongoDB image with the tag 3.4.4 available for use.

In step 3, we start a container in detached (`-d`) mode. As all containers use ephemeral storage and as we wish to retain the data, we mount a volume (`-v`) by providing it a local path `/data/db` that can be mounted to the container's internal directory `/data/db`. This ensures that even if the container is stopped/removed, our data on the host machine is retained on the host's `/data/db` path. At this point, one could also use Docker's volumes, but in order to keep things simplified, I prefer using a regular directory. Next, in the command we provide a name (`--name`) for our container. This is followed by the Docker image and tag that should be used to run the container, in our case it would be `mongo:3.4.4`. When you enter the command, you should get a large string as a return value, this is your new container's ID.

Installation and Configuration

In step 4, we run the `docker ps` command which shows us a list of running containers. If, in case your container is stopped or exited, use `docker ps -a` to show all containers. In the output you can see the container's details. By default, Docker starts a container in bridge mode that is, when Docker is installed, it creates a bridge interface on the host and the resulting containers are run using a virtual network device attached to the bridge. This results in complete network isolation of the container. Thus, in our case, if we wish to connect to the container's mongod instance on `27017`, we would need to explicitly expose TCP port `27017` to the base host or bind the base host's port to that of the container thus allowing an external MongoDB client to connect to our instance. You can read more about Docker's networking architecture at https://docs.docker.com/engine/userguide/networking/.

In step 5, we execute the mongo shell command from the container to connect to the *mongod* instance. The official MongoDB container image also takes in command-line flags, by passing them in the `docker run` command. We do this in step 6 along with running the container in host mode networking. Host mode networking binds the server's network namespace onto the container thus bypassing the bridge interface. We pass the `--bind_ip` and `--port` flags to the `docker run` command which instructs mongod to bind to `127.0.0.1:27000`. As we are using host mode networking, the mongod daemon would effectively bind to the base host's loopback interface. In step 7, we connect to our new MongoDB instance but this time we explicitly provide the connection address.

There's more..

If you ever wish to debug the container, you can always run the container in the foreground by passing the `-it` parameters in place of `-d`. Additionally, try running the following command and check the output:

```
docker logs mymongo
```

Lastly, I would suggest you have a look at the start scripts used by this container's image to understand how configurations are templatized. It will definitely give you some pointers that will help when you are setting up your own MongoDB container.

Installation and Configuration

With this recipe, we conclude this chapter. I hope these recipes have helped you gear up for getting started with MongoDB. As all things go, no amount of text can replace actual practice. So I sincerely request you to get your hands dirty and attempt these recipes yourself.

In the next chapter, we will take a closer look at MongoDB's indexes and how they can be leveraged to gain a tremendous performance boost in data retrieval.

2
Understanding and Managing Indexes

In this chapter, we will be covering the following topics:

- Creating an index
- Managing existing indexes
- How to use compound indexes
- Creating background indexes
- Creating TTL-based indexes
- Creating a sparse index
- Creating a partial index
- Creating a unique index

Introduction

In this chapter, we are going to look at how to create and manage database indexes in MongoDB. We will also look at how to view index sizes, create background indexes and creating various forms of indexes. So let's get started!

Creating an index

In this recipe, we will be using a fairly large dataset and add it into MongoDB. Then we will examine how a query executes in this dataset with and without an index.

Getting ready

Assuming that you are already running a MongoDB server, we will be importing a dataset of around 100,000 records available in the form of a CSV file called `chapter_2_mock_data.csv`. You can download this file from the Packt website.

1. Import the sample data to the MongoDB server:

   ```
   $mongoimport --headerline --ignoreBlanks --type=csv -d mydb -c mockdata -h localhost chapter_2_mock_data.csv
   ```

   You should see output like this:

   ```
   2017-06-18T08:25:08.444+0530    connected to: localhost
   2017-06-18T08:25:09.498+0530 imported 100000 documents
   ```

2. Connect to the MongoDB instance and open a mongo shell:

   ```
   mongo localhost:27017
   ```

3. Check that the documents are in the right place:

   ```
   use mydb
   db.mockdata.count()
   ```

   You should see the following result:

   ```
   105000
   ```

4. Let's fetch a document with the `explain()` method:

   ```
   > db.mockdata.find({city:'Singapore'}).explain("executionStats")
   ```

   You should see the following result:

   ```
   {
       "executionStats": {
           "executionStages": {
               "advanced": 1,
               "direction": "forward",
               "docsExamined": 100000,
               "executionTimeMillisEstimate": 44,
               "filter": {
                   "city": {
                       "$eq": "Singapore"
                   }
               },
   ```

```
                "invalidates": 0,
                "isEOF": 1,
                "nReturned": 1,
                "needTime": 100000,
                "needYield": 0,
                "restoreState": 783,
                "saveState": 783,
                "stage": "COLLSCAN",
                "works": 100002
            },
            "executionSuccess": true,
            "executionTimeMillis": 41,
            "nReturned": 1,
            "totalDocsExamined": 100000,
            "totalKeysExamined": 0
        },
        "ok": 1,
        "queryPlanner": {
            "indexFilterSet": false,
            "namespace": "mydb.mockdata",
            "parsedQuery": {
                "city": {
                    "$eq": "Singapore"
                }
            },
            "plannerVersion": 1,
            "rejectedPlans": [],
            "winningPlan": {
                "direction": "forward",
                "filter": {
                    "city": {
                        "$eq": "Singapore"
                    }
                },
                "stage": "COLLSCAN"
            }
        },
        "serverInfo": {
            "gitVersion":
"888390515874a9debd1b6c5d36559ca86b44babd",
            "host": "vagrant-ubuntu-trusty-64",
            "port": 27017,
            "version": "3.4.4"
        }
    }
```

Understanding and Managing Indexes

5. Create an index on the `city` field:

   ```
   > db.mockdata.createIndex({'city': 1})
   ```

   The following result is obtained:

   ```
   {
     "createdCollectionAutomatically" : false,
     "numIndexesBefore" : 1,
     "numIndexesAfter" : 2,
     "ok" : 1
   }
   ```

6. Execute the same fetch query:

   ```
   > db.mockdata.find({city:'Singapore'}).explain("executionStats")
   {
       "executionStats": {
           "executionStages": {
               "advanced": 1,
               "alreadyHasObj": 0,
               "docsExamined": 1,
               "executionTimeMillisEstimate": 0,
               "inputStage": {
                   "advanced": 1,
                   "direction": "forward",
                   "dupsDropped": 0,
                   "dupsTested": 0,
                   "executionTimeMillisEstimate": 0,
                   "indexBounds": {
                       "city": [
                           "[\"Singapore\", \"Singapore\"]"
                       ]
                   },
                   "indexName": "city_1",
                   "indexVersion": 2,
                   "invalidates": 0,
                   "isEOF": 1,
                   "isMultiKey": false,
                   "isPartial": false,
                   "isSparse": false,
                   "isUnique": false,
                   "keyPattern": {
                       "city": 1
                   },
                   "keysExamined": 1,
                   "multiKeyPaths": {
   ```

```
                                "city": []
                            },
                            "nReturned": 1,
                            "needTime": 0,
                            "needYield": 0,
                            "restoreState": 0,
                            "saveState": 0,
                            "seeks": 1,
                            "seenInvalidated": 0,
                            "stage": "IXSCAN",
                            "works": 2
                        },
                        "invalidates": 0,
                        "isEOF": 1,
                        "nReturned": 1,
                        "needTime": 0,
                        "needYield": 0,
                        "restoreState": 0,
                        "saveState": 0,
                        "stage": "FETCH",
                        "works": 2
                    },
                    "executionSuccess": true,
                    "executionTimeMillis": 0,
                    "nReturned": 1,
                    "totalDocsExamined": 1,
                    "totalKeysExamined": 1
                },
                "ok": 1,
                "queryPlanner": {
                    "indexFilterSet": false,
                    "namespace": "mydb.mockdata",
                    "parsedQuery": {
                        "city": {
                            "$eq": "Singapore"
                        }
                    },
                    "plannerVersion": 1,
                    "rejectedPlans": [],
                    "winningPlan": {
                        "inputStage": {
                            "direction": "forward",
                            "indexBounds": {
                                "city": [
                                    "[\"Singapore\", \"Singapore\"]"
                                ]
                            },
                            "indexName": "city_1",
```

```
                        "indexVersion": 2,
                        "isMultiKey": false,
                        "isPartial": false,
                        "isSparse": false,
                        "isUnique": false,
                        "keyPattern": {
                            "city": 1
                        },
                        "multiKeyPaths": {
                            "city": []
                        },
                        "stage": "IXSCAN"
                    },
                    "stage": "FETCH"
                }
            },
            "serverInfo": {
                "gitVersion": "888390515874a9debd1b6c5d36559ca86b44babd",
                "host": "vagrant-ubuntu-trusty-64",
                "port": 27017,
                "version": "3.4.4"
            }
        }
```

How it works...

In step 1, we used the `mongoimport` utility to import our sample dataset from `chapter_2_mock_data.csv` which is a comma separated file. We'll discuss more about `mongoimport` in later chapters, so don't worry about it for now. Once we import the data, we execute the mongo shell and confirm that we've indeed imported our sample dataset (100,000 documents).

In step 4, we run a simple `find()` function chained with the `explain()` function. The `explain()` function shows us all the details about the execution of our query, especially the `executionStats`. In this, if you look at the value of key `executionStages['stage']`, you can see it says COLLSAN. This indicates that the entire collection was scanned, which can be confirmed by looking at the `totalDocsExamined` key's value, which should say 100,000. Clearly our collection needs an index!

In step 5, we create and index by calling `db.mockdata.createIndex({'city': 1})`. In `createIndex()` function, we mention the `city` field with value of 1 which tells MongoDB to create an ascending index on this key. You can use -1 to create a descending index, if need be. By executing this function, MongoDB immediately begins creating an index on the collection.

> Index creation is an intensive blocking call which means database operations will be blocked until the index is created. We will examine how to create background indexes in later recipes, in this chapter.

In step 6, we execute the exact same `find()` query, as we did in step 4, and upon inspecting the `executionStats`, you can observe that the value of key `executionStages` now contains some more details. Especially, the value of stage key is `FETCH` and the `inputStages['stage']` is `IXSCAN`. In short, this indicates that the query was fetched from by running an index scan. As this was a direct index hit, the value of `totalDocsExamined` is 1.

There's more...

Over time, you may come across scenarios that require redesigning your indexing strategy. This may be by adding a new feature in your application or simply by identifying a more appropriate key that can be indexed. In either case, it is highly advisable to remove older (unused) indexes to ensure you do not have any unnecessary overhead on the database.

> In order to remove an index, you can use the `db.<collection>.dropIndex(<index_name>)`. If you are not sure about your index name, use the `db.<collection>.getIndexes()` function.

Managing existing indexes

In this recipe, we will be looking at some common operations we can perform on indexes like viewing, deleting, checking index sizes, and re-indexing.

Understanding and Managing Indexes

Getting ready

For this recipe, load the sample dataset and create an index on the `city` field, as described in the previous recipe.

How to do it...

1. We begin by connecting to the mongo shell of the server and viewing all indexes on the system:

    ```
    > db.mockdata.getIndexes()
    ```

    The following result is obtained:

    ```
    [
      {
        "v" : 2,
        "key" : {
          "_id" : 1
        },
        "name" : "_id_",
        "ns" : "mydb.mockdata"
      },
      {
        "v" : 2,
        "key" : {
          "city" : 1,
          "first_name" : 1
        },
        "name" : "city_1_first_name_1",
        "ns" : "mydb.mockdata"
      }
    ]
    ```

2. Execute a `dropIndex()` command to delete a particular index:

    ```
    > db.mockdata.dropIndex('city_1_first_name_1')
    ```

    You should see the following result:

    ```
    { "nIndexesWas" : 2, "ok" : 1 }
    ```

3. Let's recreate the index:

   ```
   > db.mockdata.createIndex({'city':1}, {name: 'city_index'})

   {
      "createdCollectionAutomatically" : false,
      "numIndexesBefore" : 1,
      "numIndexesAfter" : 2,
      "ok" : 1
   }
   ```

4. Run `getIndexes()` to fetch all indexes of the collection:

   ```
   > db.mockdata.getIndexes()
   ```

   We should see the following result:

   ```
   [
     {
       "v" : 2,
       "key" : {
         "_id" : 1
       },
       "name" : "_id_",
       "ns" : "mydb.mockdata"
     },
     {
       "v" : 2,
       "key" : {
         "city" : 1
       },
       "name" : "city_index",
       "ns" : "mydb.mockdata"
     }
   ]
   ```

5. Try creating the index again on the `city` field:

   ```
   > db.mockdata.createIndex({'city':1})
   ```

[37]

Understanding and Managing Indexes

You should see the following message:

```
{
  "createdCollectionAutomatically" : false,
  "numIndexesBefore" : 2,
  "numIndexesAfter" : 2,
  "note" : "all indexes already exist",
  "ok" : 1
}
```

6. Check the size of the index:

```
stats = db.mockdata.stats()
stats["totalIndexSize"]
```

It should show the following result:

```
1818624
```

7. Let us view the size of each index:

```
stats["indexSizes"]
```

This should show the following result:

```
{ "_id_" : 905216, "city_index" : 913408 }
```

8. Re-index `city_index`:

```
> db.mockdata.reIndex('city_index')
```

The following result is obtained:

```
{
  "nIndexesWas" : 2,
  "nIndexes" : 2,
  "indexes" : [
    {
      "v" : 2,
      "key" : {
        "_id" : 1
      },
      "name" : "_id_",
      "ns" : "mydb.mockdata"
    },
    {
      "v" : 2,
```

[38]

```
          "key" : {
            "city" : 1
          },
          "name" : "city_index",
          "ns" : "mydb.mockdata"
        }
      ],
      "ok" : 1
    }
```

How it works...

Most of the commands are pretty self-explanatory. In steps 1 and 2, we view and delete index respectively. You can also use `db.<collection>.dropIndexes()` to delete all indexes. In step 3, we recreate the index on the `city` field, but this time we provide an additional parameter to customize the name of the index. This can be confirmed by viewing the output of the `getIndexes()` command, as shown in step 3. Next, in step 4, we try to create another index on the `city` field (in ascending order). However, as we already have an index on this field, this would be redundant and hence MongoDB does not allow it. If you change the 1 to -1 that is, change the sort order to descending, then your operation would succeed and you'd end up with another index on the `city` field, but sorted in descending order.

In step 5, we run the `stats()` function on the collection which can alternately be run as `db.mockdata.runCommand('collstats')` and save its output in a temporary variable called stats. If we inspect the `totalIndexSize` and `indexSizes` keys, we can find the total as well as index specific sizes, respectively. At this point, I would strongly suggest you have a look at other keys in the output. It should give you a peek into the low-level internals of how MongoDB manages each collection.

Lastly, in step 6, we re-index an existing index. In that, it drops the existing index and rebuilds it either in the foreground or background, depending on how it was set up initially. It is usually not necessary to rebuild the index, however, as per MongoDB's documentation you may choose to do so if you feel that the index size may be disproportionate or your collection has significantly grown in size.

How to use compound indexes

The beauty of indexes is that they can be used with multiple keys. A single key index can be thought of as a table with one column. A multi-key index or compound index can be visualized as a multi column table where the first column is sorted first, and then the next, and so on. In this recipe, we will look at how to create a compound index and examine how it works.

Getting ready

Load the sample dataset and create an index on the `city` field, as described in the previous recipe.

How to do it...

1. Assuming you have already created an index on the `city` field, create one by executing the command `db.mockdata.createIndex({'city': 1})` again.
2. Run a `find()` query:

    ```
    > plan = db.mockdata.find({city:'Boston', first_name:'Sara'}).explain("executionStats")
    ```

3. Examine the `executionStats`:

    ```
    > plan['executionStats']
    ```

    You should see the following result:

    ```
    {
      "executionSuccess" : true,
      "nReturned" : 1,
      "executionTimeMillis" : 0,
      "totalKeysExamined" : 9,
      "totalDocsExamined" : 9,
      "executionStages" : {
        "stage" : "FETCH",
        "filter" : {
          "first_name" : {
            "$eq" : "Sara"
          }
        },
        "nReturned" : 1,
    ```

```
            "executionTimeMillisEstimate" : 0,
            "works" : 10,
            "advanced" : 1,
            "needTime" : 8,
            "needYield" : 0,
            "saveState" : 0,
            "restoreState" : 0,
            "isEOF" : 1,
            "invalidates" : 0,
            "docsExamined" : 9,
            "alreadyHasObj" : 0,
            "inputStage" : {
              "stage" : "IXSCAN",
              "nReturned" : 9,
              "executionTimeMillisEstimate" : 0,
              "works" : 10,
              "advanced" : 9,
              "needTime" : 0,
              "needYield" : 0,
              "saveState" : 0,
              "restoreState" : 0,
              "isEOF" : 1,
              "invalidates" : 0,
              "keyPattern" : {
                "city" : 1
              },
              "indexName" : "city_1",
              "isMultiKey" : false,
              "multiKeyPaths" : {
                "city" : [ ]
              },
              "isUnique" : false,
              "isSparse" : false,
              "isPartial" : false,
              "indexVersion" : 2,
              "direction" : "forward",
              "indexBounds" : {
                "city" : [
                  "[\"Boston\", \"Boston\"]"
                ]
              },
              "keysExamined" : 9,
              "seeks" : 1,
              "dupsTested" : 0,
              "dupsDropped" : 0,
              "seenInvalidated" : 0
          }
        }
```

Understanding and Managing Indexes

   }

4. Now drop this index:

   ```
   > db.mockdata.dropIndex('city_1')
   ```

   You should see an output similar to this:

   ```
   { "nIndexesWas" : 2, "ok" : 1 }
   ```

5. Create a compound index on city and name:

   ```
   > db.mockdata.createIndex({'city': 1, 'first_name': 1})
   ```

   You should see an output similar to this:

   ```
   {
   "createdCollectionAutomatically" : false,
   "numIndexesBefore" : 1,
   "numIndexesAfter" : 2,
   "ok" : 1
   }
   ```

6. Let's run the same fetch query again and examine the plan:

   ```
   > plan = db.mockdata.find({city:'Boston', first_name:
   'Sara'}).explain("executionStats")

   > plan['executionStats']
   ```

   You should see an output similar to this:

   ```
   {
     "executionSuccess": true,
     "nReturned": 1,
     "executionTimeMillis": 0,
     "totalKeysExamined": 1,
     "totalDocsExamined": 1,
     "executionStages": {
       "stage": "FETCH",
       "nReturned": 1,
       "executionTimeMillisEstimate": 0,
       "works": 2,
       "advanced": 1,
       "needTime": 0,
       "needYield": 0,
       "saveState": 0,
       "restoreState": 0,
   ```

```
            "isEOF": 1,
            "invalidates": 0,
            "docsExamined": 1,
            "alreadyHasObj": 0,
            "inputStage": {
              "stage": "IXSCAN",
              "nReturned": 1,
              "executionTimeMillisEstimate": 0,
              "works": 2,
              "advanced": 1,
              "needTime": 0,
              "needYield": 0,
              "saveState": 0,
              "restoreState": 0,
              "isEOF": 1,
              "invalidates": 0,
              "keyPattern": {
                "city": 1,
                "first_name": 1
              },
              "indexName": "city_1_first_name_1",
              "isMultiKey": false,
              "multiKeyPaths": {
                "city": [],
                "first_name": []
              },
              "isUnique": false,
              "isSparse": false,
              "isPartial": false,
              "indexVersion": 2,
              "direction": "forward",
              "indexBounds": {
                "city": [
                  "[\"Boston\", \"Boston\"]"
                ],
                "first_name": [
                  "[\"Sara\", \"Sara\"]"
                ]
              },
              "keysExamined": 1,
              "seeks": 1,
              "dupsTested": 0,
              "dupsDropped": 0,
              "seenInvalidated": 0
            }
          }
        }
```

How it works...

We start with loading the sample dataset with an index on the `city` field. Next, we execute a `find()` command on our collection chained with the `explain('executionStats')` function, in steps 2 and 3 respectively. This time, we capture the output of the data in a variable so it is easier to examine for later use.

In step 4, we specifically examine the execution stats. We can observe that nine documents were fetched from the index in which we had one match. When we ran `db.mockdata.find({city:'Boston', first_name: 'Sara'})`, MongoDB first saw that the `city` field already has an index on it. So, for the remaining part of the query, MongoDB simply searched the documents which were returned from the index and searched on the field `first_name` in these documents until they matched the value `Sara`.

In step 5, we remove the existing index on field `city` and in step 6, we create a compound index on two field names `city` and `first_name`. At this point, I would like to point, that the sequence of the field names is extremely important. As I explained in the introduction of this recipe, compound indexes in MongoDB are created in the order in which the field names are mentioned. Hence, when we create a compound index with, say, `{city:1, first_name:1}`, MongoDB first creates a B-tree index on the field `city` and an ascending order followed by `first_name` in an ascending order.

In step 7, we run the same `find()` query and examine the `executionStats`. We can observe that this time, as both keys were indexed, `totalDocumentsExamined` was 1 that is, we got an exact match in our compound index.

There's more...

Compound indexes, if used smartly, can dramatically reduce your document seek times. For example, let's assume our application had a view that only required us to show a list of names in a city. A traditional approach would be to run a find query and get the list of documents and send them to the application's view. However, we know that other fields in the document are not needed for this view. Then, by having a compound index on `city` and `first_name` with the addition of field projection, we simply send the index values down to the application that is:

```
db.mockdata.find({city:'Boston', first_name:'Sara'}, {city:1, first_name:1, _id:0})
```

By doing this, not only do we leverage the speed of the index but we negate the need to fetch the non-indexed keys. Another term used for this is a covered query and it can improve our applications significantly!

Also, compound indexes allow us to use the index for the leftmost key. In our example, if we were to run `db.mockdata.find({city:'Boston'})`, then the result would be fetched from the index. However, if we were to search on the first_name that is, `db.mockdata.find({first_name:'Sara'})`, the server would do a full collection scan and fetch the result. I would encourage you to run the preceding queries chained with the `explain()` function and see the details yourself.

Creating background indexes

In the previous recipes, whenever we've created indexes, it has always been in the foreground that is, the database server blocks all changes to the database until the index creation is completed. This is definitely not suitable for larger datasets where index creation time can take a few seconds which could be application errors.

Getting ready

Load the sample dataset, as shown in the *Creating an index* recipe.

How to do it...

1. Remove all indexes:

   ```
   > db.mockdata.dropIndexes()
   
   {
       "nIndexesWas" : 2,
       "msg" : "non-_id indexes dropped for collection",
       "ok" : 1
   }
   ```

2. Add some additional data to increase the size of our collection. Run the following command string in your Terminal window:

   ```
   for x in $(seq 20); do mongoimport --headerline --type=csv -d mydb -c mockdata -h localhost chapter_2_mock_data.csv;done
   ```

Understanding and Managing Indexes

3. Open two mongo shells, we will create an index in one while we do an insert query in another. Ensure you've selected `mydb` by executing the command `use mydb` in both windows.
4. In the first mongo shell, create an index and immediately shift to the second shell:

    ```
    > db.mockdata.createIndex({city:1, first_name:1, last_name:1})
    ```

5. In the second shell window, perform a simple insert operation:

    ```
    > db.mockdata.insert({foo:'bar'})
    ```

6. Check the mongod server logs:

    ```
    2017-06-13T03:54:26.296+0000 I INDEX [conn1] build index on:
    mydb.mockdata properties: { v: 2, key: { city: 1.0, first_name:
    1.0, last_name: 1.0 }, name: "city_1_first_name_1_last_name_1", ns:
    "mydb.mockdata" }
    2017-06-13T03:54:26.297+0000 I INDEX [conn1] building index using
    bulk method; build may temporarily use up to 500 megabytes of RAM
     2017-06-13T03:54:36.575+0000 I INDEX [conn1] build index done.
    scanned 2100001 total records. 10 secs
     2017-06-13T03:54:36.576+0000 I COMMAND [conn2] command
    mydb.mockdata appName: "MongoDB Shell" command: insert { insert:
    "mockdata", documents: [ { _id:
    ObjectId('59474af356e41a7db57952b6'), foo: "bar" } ], ordered: true
    } ninserted:1 keysInserted:3 numYields:0 reslen:29 locks:{ Global:
    { acquireCount: { r: 1, w: 1 } }, Database: { acquireCount: { w: 1
    }, acquireWaitCount: { w: 1 }, timeAcquiringMicros: { w: 9307131 }
    }, Collection: { acquireCount: { w: 1 } } } protocol:op_command
    9307ms
     2017-06-13T03:54:36.577+0000 I COMMAND [conn1] command mydb.$cmd
    appName: "MongoDB Shell" command: createIndexes { createIndexes:
    "mockdata", indexes: [ { key: { city: 1.0, first_name: 1.0,
    last_name: 1.0 }, name: "city_1_first_name_1_last_name_1" } ] }
    numYields:0 reslen:98 locks:{ Global: { acquireCount: { r: 1, w: 1
    } }, Database: { acquireCount: { W: 1 } }, Collection: {
    acquireCount: { w: 1 } } } protocol:op_command 10284ms
    ```

7. Now drop the indexes and get ready to repeat steps 4 and step 5 again.
8. In the first mongo shell window, recreate the index. As this command will take some time, switch to the second shell window:

    ```
    > db.mockdata.createIndex({city:1, first_name:1, last_name:1},
    {background:1})
    ```

9. In the second shell window, perform an insert operation, this time it should immediately yield:

   ```
   > db.mockdata.insert({foo:'bar'})
   ```

   You should see the following output:

   ```
   WriteResult({ "nInserted" : 1 })
   ```

10. Look at the mongod server logs:

    ```
    2017-06-13T04:00:29.248+0000 I INDEX [conn1] build index on:
    mydb.mockdata properties: { v: 2, key: { city: 1.0, first_name:
    1.0, last_name: 1.0 }, name: "city_1_first_name_1_last_name_1", ns:
    "mydb.mockdata", background: 1.0 }
    2017-06-13T04:00:32.008+0000 I - [conn1] Index Build (background):
    397400/2200004 18%
     2017-06-13T04:00:35.002+0000 I - [conn1] Index Build (background):
    673800/2200005 30%
     2017-06-13T04:00:38.009+0000 I - [conn1] Index Build (background):
    762300/2200005 34%
     2017-06-13T04:00:41.006+0000 I - [conn1] Index Build (background):
    903400/2200005 41%
     << --- output snipped --- >>
     2123200/2200005 96%
     2017-06-13T04:02:32.021+0000 I - [conn1] Index Build (background):
    2148300/2200005 97%
     2017-06-13T04:02:35.021+0000 I - [conn1] Index Build (background):
    2172800/2200005 98%
     2017-06-13T04:02:38.019+0000 I - [conn1] Index Build (background):
    2195800/2200005 99%
     2017-06-13T04:02:38.566+0000 I INDEX [conn1] build index done.
    scanned 2100006 total records. 129 secs
     2017-06-13T04:02:38.572+0000 I COMMAND [conn1] command mydb.$cmd
    appName: "MongoDB Shell" command: createIndexes { createIndexes:
    "mockdata", indexes: [ { key: { city: 1.0, first_name: 1.0,
    last_name: 1.0 }, name: "city_1_first_name_1_last_name_1",
    background: 1.0 } ] } numYields:20353 reslen:98 locks:{ Global: {
    acquireCount: { r: 20354, w: 20354 } }, Database: { acquireCount: {
    w: 20354, W: 2 } }, Collection: { acquireCount: { w: 20354 } } }
    protocol:op_command 129326ms
    ```

Understanding and Managing Indexes

How it works...

In step 1 we remove any existing indexes. Next, in order to better simulate index creation delays, what we do is simply keep reimporting our sample dataset about 20 times. This should give us about 2 million records in our collection after the end of step 2. As I have the previous recipes' sample dataset, my document count may be slightly higher so don't worry about it.

Now, in order to test how foreground index creation hinders database operations, we need to be able to perform two tasks simultaneously. For this, we set up two terminal windows, preferably side by side, with mongo shells connected and ensure `mydb` is selected. In step 4, we create a index on three fields `city`, `first_name`, and `last_name`. Again, this is intentional to add a bit of computational overhead for our test database setup. Note that, unlike previous runs, this command will not yield immediately. So, switch to the next terminal windows and try inserting a simple record, as shown in step 5. If you have both window stacked side by side, you will notice that both of them yield almost simultaneously. If you look at mongod server logs, you can see that both operations, in this case, took roughly 10 seconds to complete. Also, as expected, our insert query did not complete until the index creation had released the lock on the collection.

In step 7, we delete the index again and in step 8 we recreate the index but this time with the option `{background: 1}`. This tells mongod to start the index creation process in the background. In step 9, we switch to the other terminal window and try inserting a random document to our collection. Lo and behold, our document gets inserted immediately. Now is a good time to switch to the mongod server logs. As shown in step 10, you can now see that the index creation is happening in small batches. When the index creation completes, you can see that mongod acquired about 20,354 locks for this process as opposed to 1, when creating index in foreground. This lock and release method allowed our insert query to go through. However, this does come with a slight trade-off. The index creation time in the background was about 130 seconds as compared to 10 seconds, when created in the foreground.

There you have it, a simple test to show the effectiveness of creating background indexes. As real-world production scenarios go, it is always safe to create indexes in the background unless you have a very strong reason otherwise.

Creating TTL-based indexes

In this recipe, we will explore the `expireAfterSeconds` property of MongoDB indexes to allow automatic deletion of documents from a collection.

Getting ready

For this recipe, all you need is a mongod instance running. We will be creating and working on a new collection called `ttlcol` in the database `mydb`.

How to do it...

1. Ensure that our collection is empty:

   ```
   db.ttlcol.drop()
   ```

2. Add 200 random documents:

   ```
   for(var x=1; x<=100; x++){
     var past = new Date()
     past.setSeconds(past.getSeconds() - (x * 60))
     // Insert a document with timestamp in the past
     var doc = {
       foo: 'bar',
       timestamp: past
     }
     db.ttlcol.insert(doc)
     // Insert a document with timestamp in the future
     var future = new Date()
     future.setSeconds(future.getSeconds() + (x * 60))
     var doc = {
       foo: 'bar',
       timestamp: future
     }
     db.ttlcol.insert(doc)
   }
   ```

3. Check that the documents were added:

   ```
   db.ttlcol.count()
   ```

4. Create an index with TTL:

    ```
    db.ttlcol.createIndex({timestamp:1}, {expireAfterSeconds: 10})
    ```

    You should see output similar to this:

    ```
    {
        "createdCollectionAutomatically" : false,
        "numIndexesBefore" : 1,
        "numIndexesAfter" : 2,
        "ok" : 1
    }
    ```

5. Wait for about a minute and check the document count:

    ```
    db.ttlcol.count()
    ```

    The number of documents returned should be lower than 200.

How it works...

In step 1, we emptied the `ttlcol` collection in `mydb` to ensure there is no old data. Next, in step 2, we ran a simple JavaScript code that adds 200 records, each having a BSON `Date()` field called `timestamp`. We added about 100 records in the past and 100 in the future each 1 minute in the past and future respectively.

Then in step 3, we created a regular index but with an additional parameter `{expireAfterSeconds: 10}`. In this, we are telling the server to expire documents 10 seconds from the value of time mentioned in our `timestamp` field. Once this is added, you can check that the number of documents in the collection has reduced from 200 to, in this case, 113 and counting. What happens here is that there is a background thread in MongoDB server that wakes up every minute and removes any document that matches our index's condition. At this point, I would like to point out that if our field `timestamp` were not a valid `Date()` function or an array of Date() function, then no documents would be removed.

There's more...

If you wish to have explicit expiry times, then set the `expireAfterSecond` to 0. In that, the documents would be removed as soon as they match the desired field's timestamp.

So when would you need a TTL-based index? Well if you happen to store time sensitive documents like user session times or documents that can be removed after a certain period like events, logs, or transaction history, then TTL-based indexes are your best option. They offer you more control over document retention than traditional capped collections.

Creating a sparse index

MongoDB allows you to create an index on fields that may not exist in all documents, in a given collection. These are called sparse indexes and in this recipe, we will look at how to create them.

Getting ready

For this recipe, load the sample dataset and create an index on the `city` field, as described in the *Creating an index* recipe.

How to do it...

1. Check the total number of documents in our collection and number of documents without the `language` field:

   db.mockdata.count()

   The preceding command should return `100000`.

   db.mockdata.find({language: {$eq:null}}).count()

   The preceding command should return `12704`.

2. Create a sparse index on the document:

   db.mockdata.createIndex({language:1}, {sparse: true})

Understanding and Managing Indexes

You should see output similar to this:

```
{
    "createdCollectionAutomatically" : false,
    "numIndexesBefore" : 1,
    "numIndexesAfter" : 2,
    "ok" : 1
}
```

3. Check our index got created with the `sparse` parameter:

```
db.mockdata.getIndexes()
```

The preceding command should give you output similar to this:

```
[
  {
    "key": {
      "_id": 1
    },
    "name": "_id_",
    "ns": "test.mockdata",
    "v": 2
  },
  {
    "key": {
      "language": 1
    },
    "name": "language_1",
    "ns": "test.mockdata",
    "sparse": true,
    "v": 2
  }
]
```

4. Run a simple `find` query:

```
db.mockdata.find({language:
'French'}).explain('executionStats')['executionStats']
```

[52]

Understanding and Managing Indexes

The preceding command should give you output similar to this:

```
"executionStages": {
    "advanced": 893,
    "alreadyHasObj": 0,
    "docsExamined": 893,
    "executionTimeMillisEstimate": 0,
    "inputStage": {
        "advanced": 893,
        "direction": "forward",
        "dupsDropped": 0,
        "dupsTested": 0,
        "executionTimeMillisEstimate": 0,
        "indexBounds": {
            "language": [
                "[\"French\", \"French\"]"
            ]
        },
        "indexName": "language_1",
        "indexVersion": 2,
        "invalidates": 0,
        "isEOF": 1,
        "isMultiKey": false,
        "isPartial": false,
        "isSparse": true,
        "isUnique": false,
        "keyPattern": {
            "language": 1
        },
        "keysExamined": 893,
        "multiKeyPaths": {
            "language": []
        },
        "nReturned": 893,
        "needTime": 0,
        "needYield": 0,
        "restoreState": 6,
        "saveState": 6,
        "seeks": 1,
        "seenInvalidated": 0,
        "stage": "IXSCAN",
        "works": 894
    },
    "invalidates": 0,
    "isEOF": 1,
    "nReturned": 893,
    "needTime": 0,
    "needYield": 0,
```

[53]

```
            "restoreState": 6,
            "saveState": 6,
            "stage": "FETCH",
            "works": 894
        },
        "executionSuccess": true,
        "executionTimeMillis": 1,
        "nReturned": 893,
        "totalDocsExamined": 893,
        "totalKeysExamined": 893
    }
```

How it works...

For this example, we have picked a sparsely populated field, `language`, which does not exist in all documents of our sample dataset. In step 1, we can see that around 12,000 documents do not contain this field. Next, in step 2, we create an index with the optional parameter `{sparse: true}` which tells MongoDB server to create a sparse index on our field, `language`. The index gets created and works just like any other index as seen in steps 3 and step 4, respectively.

Creating a partial index

Partial indexes were introduced recently, in MongoDB Version 3.2. A partial index is slightly similar to sparse index but with the added advantage of being able to use expressions ($eq, $gt, and so on) and operators ($and).

Getting ready

For this recipe, load the sample dataset and create an index on the `city` field, as described in the *Creating an index* recipe.

How to do it...

1. Check the total number of documents in our collection and number of documents without the `language` field:

   ```
   db.mockdata.count()
   ```

Understanding and Managing Indexes

The preceding command should return `100000`:

```
db.mockdata.find({language: {$eq:null}}).count()
```

The preceding command should return `12704`.

2. Create a sparse index on the document:

```
> db.mockdata.createIndex(
  {first_name:1},
  {partialFilterExpression: { language: {$exists: true}}}
)
```

This should give you output similar to this:

```
{
        "createdCollectionAutomatically" : false,
        "numIndexesBefore" : 1,
        "numIndexesAfter" : 2,
        "ok" : 1
}
```

3. Confirm that the index was created:

```
db.mockdata.getIndexes()
```

The preceding command should give you output similar to this:

```
[
  {
    "key": {
      "_id": 1
    },
    "name": "_id_",
    "ns": "mydb.mockdata",
    "v": 2
  },
  {
    "key": {
      "first_name": 1
    },
    "name": "first_name_1",
    "ns": "mydb.mockdata",
    "partialFilterExpression": {
      "language": {
        "$exists": true
      }
    },
```

Understanding and Managing Indexes

```
            "v": 2
        }
    ]
```

4. Find a record without `language` field:

   ```
   db.mockdata.find({first_name:
   'Sara'}).explain('executionStats')['executionStats']
   ```

   The preceding command should give you output similar to this:

   ```
   {
     "executionStages": {
       "advanced": 7,
       "direction": "forward",
       "docsExamined": 100000,
       "executionTimeMillisEstimate": 21,
       "filter": {
         "first_name": {
           "$eq": "Sara"
         }
       },
       "invalidates": 0,
       "isEOF": 1,
       "nReturned": 7,
       "needTime": 99994,
       "needYield": 0,
       "restoreState": 782,
       "saveState": 782,
       "stage": "COLLSCAN",
       "works": 100002
     },
     "executionSuccess": true,
     "executionTimeMillis": 33,
     "nReturned": 7,
     "totalDocsExamined": 100000,
     "totalKeysExamined": 0
   }
   ```

5. Find a record with `language` field:

   ```
   db.mockdata.find({first_name: 'Sara', language:
   'Spanish'}).explain('executionStats')['executionStats']
   ```

Understanding and Managing Indexes

The preceding command should give you output similar to this:

```
{
  "executionStages": {
    "advanced": 1,
    "alreadyHasObj": 0,
    "docsExamined": 7,
    "executionTimeMillisEstimate": 0,
    "filter": {
      "language": {
        "$eq": "Spanish"
      }
    },
    "inputStage": {
      "advanced": 7,
      "direction": "forward",
      "dupsDropped": 0,
      "dupsTested": 0,
      "executionTimeMillisEstimate": 0,
      "indexBounds": {
        "first_name": [
          "[\"Sara\", \"Sara\"]"
        ]
      },
      "indexName": "first_name_1",
      "indexVersion": 2,
      "invalidates": 0,
      "isEOF": 1,
      "isMultiKey": false,
      "isPartial": true,
      "isSparse": false,
      "isUnique": false,
      "keyPattern": {
        "first_name": 1
      },
      "keysExamined": 7,
      "multiKeyPaths": {
        "first_name": []
      },
      "nReturned": 7,
      "needTime": 0,
      "needYield": 0,
      "restoreState": 0,
      "saveState": 0,
      "seeks": 1,
      "seenInvalidated": 0,
      "stage": "IXSCAN",
      "works": 8
```

```
            },
            "invalidates": 0,
            "isEOF": 1,
            "nReturned": 1,
            "needTime": 6,
            "needYield": 0,
            "restoreState": 0,
            "saveState": 0,
            "stage": "FETCH",
            "works": 8
        },
        "executionSuccess": true,
        "executionTimeMillis": 0,
        "nReturned": 1,
        "totalDocsExamined": 7,
        "totalKeysExamined": 7
    }
```

How it works...

As in the previous recipe, we have picked a sparsely populated field, language, which does not exist in all documents of our sample dataset. In step 1, we can see that around 12,000 documents do not contain this field.

Next, in step 2, we create an index on the field first_name with the optional parameter partialFilterExpression. With this parameter, we have added a condition { language: {$exists: true}}. MongoDB is instructed to create an index on first_name only on documents which have the field language present. If we look at the executionStats in step 4, we can observe that the index is not used if we do a simple search on the field first_name. However, in step 5, we can see that our query is using the MongoDB index if we add an additional parameter of the field language.

Apart from this simple example, there are tons of good variations possible if we use expressions like $lt, $gt, and so on. You can find some more examples at https://docs.mongodb.com/manual/core/index-partial/.

So why would one use a partial index? Say, for example, you have a huge dataset and wish to have an index on a field which is sparsely spread across these documents. Traditional indexes would cause the entire collection to be indexed and may not be optimal if we are going to work on a subset of these documents.

Creating a unique index

MongoDB allows you to create an index on a field with the option of ensuring that it is unique in the collection. In this recipe, we will explore how it can be done.

Getting ready

For this recipe, we only need a running mongod instance.

How to do it...

1. Connect to the mongo shell and insert a random document:

   ```
   use mydb
   db.testuniq.insert({foo: 'zoidberg'})
   ```

2. Create an index with the unique parameter:

   ```
   db.testuniq.createIndex({foo:1}, {unique:1})
   ```

   The preceding command should give you an output similar to this:

   ```
   {
     "createdCollectionAutomatically": false,
     "numIndexesAfter": 2,
     "numIndexesBefore": 1,
     "ok": 1
   }
   ```

3. Try to add another document with a duplicate value of the field:

   ```
   db.testuniq.insert({foo: 'zoidberg'})
   ```

Understanding and Managing Indexes

The preceding command should give you an error message similar to this:

```
WriteResult({
  "nInserted" : 0,
  "writeError" : {
    "code" : 11000,
    "errmsg" : "E11000 duplicate key error collection:
mydb.testuniq index: foo_1 dup key: { : \"zoidberg\" }"
  }
})
```

4. Drop the index:

```
db.testuniq.dropIndexes()
```

5. Add a duplicate record:

```
db.testuniq.insert({foo: 'zoidberg'})
db.testuniq.find()
```

The preceding command should give you an output similar to this:

```
{ "_id" : ObjectId("59490cabc14da1366d83254f"), "foo" : "zoidberg"
}
{ "_id" : ObjectId("59490d20c14da1366d832551"), "foo" : "zoidberg"
}
```

6. Try creating the index again:

```
db.testuniq.createIndex({foo:1}, {unique:1})
```

The preceding command should give you an output similar to this:

```
{
  "ok" : 0,
  "errmsg" : "E11000 duplicate key error collection: mydb.testuniq
index: foo_1 dup key: { : \"zoidberg\" }",
  "code" : 11000,
  "codeName" : "DuplicateKey"
}
```

How it works...

In step 1 we inserted a document in a new collection `testuniq`. Next, in step 2, we created an index on the field foo with the parameter `{unique: true}`. In step 3, we try to add another record with the same value of field foo as we did earlier and we receive an error as expected.

In step 4, we drop the indexes and add a duplicate record. Next we try to create a new unique index. This time we are not allowed because there are duplicates in our collection.

This is a simple example of how to create an index with unique constraint. Additionally, we can also create unique indexes on fields that have an array, for example `{foo: ['bar', 'baz']}`. MongoDB would inspect each value of the array and against the index. Try adding a document with the above values and see what happens.

> **TIP**
>
> If you insert a document where the indexed field is missing, then MongoDB will not allow you to add another one with the indexed field missing. The missing field is considered a null value and because of the unique constraint to the index, only one field can be null.

3
Performance Tuning

In this chapter we will be covering the following topics:

- Configuring disks for better I/O
- Measuring disk I/O performance with mongoperf
- Finding slow running queries and operations
- Figuring out the size of a working set

Introduction

This chapter is slightly different than the previous ones in that we will be looking at different technical aspects that should be considered to gain optimal performance from a MongoDB setup. As you are probably aware, application performance tuning is a highly nuanced art, hence not all aspects will be covered here. However, I will try and discuss the most important points, which will help pave the way for more critical thinking on the subject.

Configuring disks for better I/O

In this recipe, we will be looking at the importance of provisioning your servers for better disk I/O.

Reading and writing from disks

Apart from CPU and memory (RAM), MongoDB, like most database applications, relies heavily on disk operations.

To better understand this dependency, let's look at a very simple example of reading data from a file. Suppose you have a file that contains a few thousand lines, each containing a set of strings in no particular order. If one were to write a program that is used to search a particular string, it would need to open the file, iterate through each line, and search the string. Once the string is found, the program closes the file. As disks are usually much slower than RAM, this approach of opening a file, reading, and closing it on every query, is suboptimal.

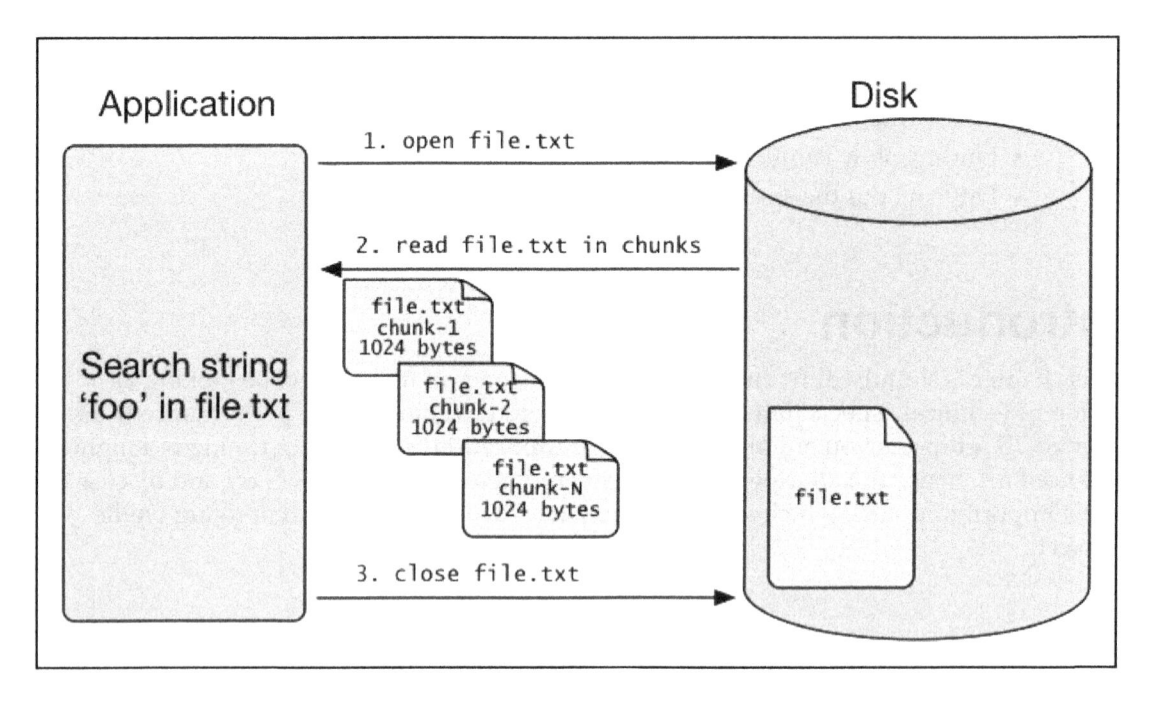

To circumvent this, Linux (and most modern operating systems) rely heavily on the cache buffer. The operating system kernel uses this cache to store chunks of data, in blocks, which are frequently read from the disk. So, when a process tries to read a particular file, the kernel first does a lookup in its cache. If the data is not cached, then the kernel reads it from the disks and loads it in the cache. Data is evicted from the cache based on its frequency of use, that is, less used data gets removed first to make room for more frequently accessed data. Additionally, the kernel tries to utilize all available free memory for the cache, but it automatically reduces the cache size if a process requires memory.

Performance Tuning

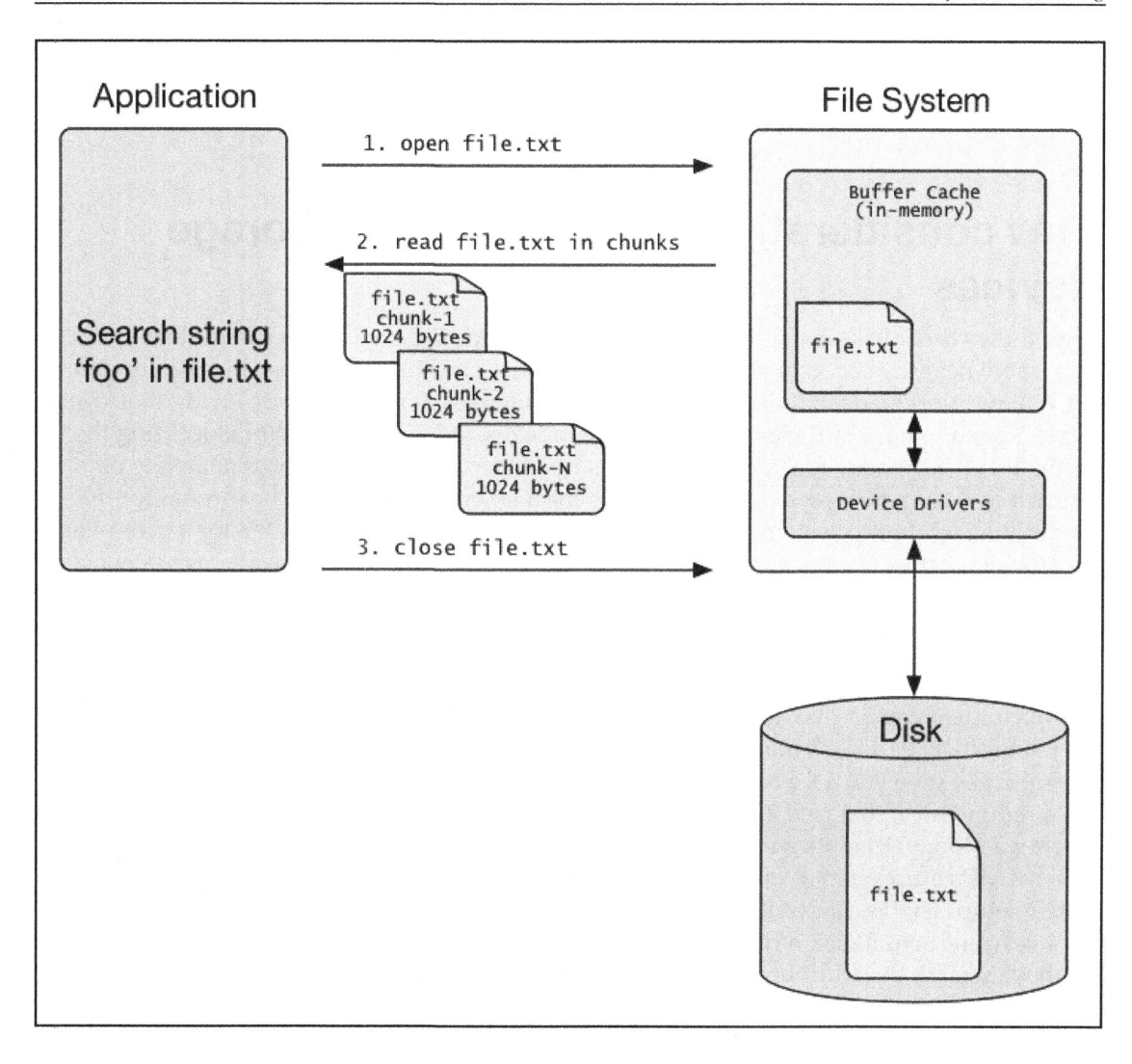

```
Application                              File System
┌──────────────┐   1. open file.txt    ┌─────────────────────┐
│              │ ────────────────────▶ │   Buffer Cache      │
│              │                       │   (in-memory)       │
│              │   2. read file.txt in chunks                │
│              │ ◀──────────────────── │   ┌──────────┐      │
│ Search string│      file.txt         │   │ file.txt │      │
│ 'foo' in     │      chunk-1          │   └──────────┘      │
│ file.txt     │      1024 bytes       │         ▲           │
│              │        file.txt       │         ▼           │
│              │        chunk-2        │   ┌──────────────┐  │
│              │        1024 bytes     │   │Device Drivers│  │
│              │          file.txt     │   └──────────────┘  │
│              │          chunk-N      │         ▲           │
│              │          1024 bytes   └─────────┼───────────┘
│              │   3. close file.txt             │
│              │ ────────────────────▶           │
└──────────────┘                                 ▼
                                          ┌──────────┐
                                          │   Disk   │
                                          │ file.txt │
                                          └──────────┘
```

The design of this cache was to circumvent the delays inherent in reading and writing on disks. Any application that relies on disk I/O would be greatly impacted by the speed of the disk. RAM, on the other hand, is extremely fast. How fast, you ask? To put it in perspective, most disk operations are in the range of milliseconds (thousands of a second), whereas for RAM, it is in nanoseconds (billionths of a second).

MongoDB is designed quite similarly to this, in that the database server tries to keep the index and the working set in memory. At the same time, for actual disk reads, it heavily relies on the filesystem buffer cache. But even with everything optimized to be in memory, at some point, MongoDB would need to either write to the disk or read from it.

Performance Tuning

Disk read/write operations are what are commonly referred to ask disk **Input/Output Operations Per Second** (**IOPS**). As disk I/O is a blocking operation, the amount of disk IOPS required by MongoDB would eventually determine how fast your database performs.

Few considerations while selecting storage devices

First things first, disks are slow. Neither magnetic nor solid state disks can perform anywhere near the speed of RAM. As MongoDB tries to store a database index in memory, try to have workloads that utilize the benefits of indexes. It goes without saying that your servers need to have sufficient RAM to store indexes and disk cache. While deciding the optimal RAM capacity for your server, consider aspects such as the percentage rate of growth of data (and indexes), sufficient size for disk buffer cache, and headroom for the underlying operating system. A very simple example for calculating IOPS for a disk would be 1/(average disk latency + average seek time). So, for a disk with 2 ms average latency and 3 ms average seek time, the total supported IOPS would be 1/(0.002 + 0.003) = 200 IOPS. Again, this does not take into account a lot of other factors, such as disk degradation, ECC, and sequential or random seeks.

With a limited cap on disk IOPS, you can substantially increase the server's IOPS capacity by using RAID 0 (disk striping). For example, an array of four disks in RAID 0 would theoretically give you 4 x 200 = 800 IOPS. The trade-off with RAID 0 is that you do not get data redundancy, that is, if a disk fails, your data is lost. But this can be easily rectified by having a MongoDB replica set. However, on the off-chance that you do decide to use any other RAID setup, keep in mind that your write operations will be directly affected by the RAID setup. That is, for RAID 1 or RAID 10 you would be performing two write operations for every one actual disk write. At the same time, RAID 5 and RAID 6 would not be suitable as they increase the additional writes even more.

Lastly, know your application requirements. I cannot stress how important it is to analyze and monitor your applications' read and write operations. It is ideal to have, at the least, a rough estimate on the ratio of reads to writes.

> Filesystems also play a crucial role. MongoDB highly recommends using the XFS filesystem. For more information, see `https://docs.mongodb.com/manual/administration/production-notes/#kernel-and-file-systems`.
> We will discuss this in the recipe 'Configuring for production deployment' in Chapter 10.

Measuring disk I/O performance with mongoperf

By now, you should have a fair idea of the importance of disk I/O and how it directly impacts your database performance. MongoDB provides a nifty little utility called mongoperf that allows us to quickly measure disk I/O performance.

Getting ready

For this recipe, we only need the mongoperf utility, which is available in the `bin` directory of your MongoDB installation.

How to do it...

1. Measure the read throughput with `mmf` disabled:

   ```
   root@ubuntu:~# echo "{ recSizeKB: 8, nThreads: 12, fileSizeMB: 10000, r: true, mmf: false }" | mongoperf
   ```

   You will get the following result:

   ```
   mongoperf use -h for help
   parsed options:
   { recSizeKB: 8, nThreads: 12, fileSizeMB: 10000, r: true, mmf: false }
   creating test file size:10000MB ...
   1GB...
   2GB...
   3GB...
   4GB...
   5GB...
   6GB...
   7GB...
   8GB...
   9GB...
   testing...
   options:{ recSizeKB: 8, nThreads: 12, fileSizeMB: 10000, r: true, mmf: false }
   wthr 12
   new thread, total running : 1
   read:1 write:0
   19789 ops/sec 77 MB/sec
   ```

Performance Tuning

```
19602 ops/sec 76 MB/sec
19173 ops/sec 74 MB/sec
19300 ops/sec 75 MB/sec
18838 ops/sec 73 MB/sec
19494 ops/sec 76 MB/sec
19579 ops/sec 76 MB/sec
19002 ops/sec 74 MB/sec
new thread, total running : 2
<---- output truncated --->
new thread, total running : 12
read:1 write:0
read:1 write:0
read:1 write:0
read:1 write:0
40544 ops/sec 158 MB/sec
40237 ops/sec 157 MB/sec
40463 ops/sec 158 MB/sec
40463 ops/sec 158 MB/sec
```

2. In another Terminal window, run `iostat` to confirm the disk utilization as follows:

```
root@ubuntu:~# iostat -mx 2
Device:     rrqm/s   wrqm/s      r/s    w/s    rMB/s   wMB/s avgrq-sz avgqu-sz   await r_await w_await  svctm  %util
sda           0.00     4.71 48250.00   1.18   376.94    0.02    16.00     2.13    0.04    0.04    0.00   0.02 105.41
sda           0.00     0.00 47483.93   0.00   370.97    0.00    16.00     2.20    0.05    0.05    0.00   0.02 107.62
sda           0.00     0.00 47495.29   0.00   371.06    0.00    16.00     2.15    0.05    0.05    0.00   0.02 107.06
```

3. Measure the read throughput with `mmf` enabled and a payload larger than the server's total memory shown as follows:

```
root@ubuntu:~# echo "{ recSizeKB: 8, nThreads: 12, fileSizeMB:
10000, r: true, mmf: true }" | mongoperf
```

The following result is obtained:

```
mongoperf
 use -h for help
 parsed options:
 { recSizeKB: 8, nThreads: 12, fileSizeMB: 10000, r: true, mmf:
true }
 creating test file size:10000MB ...
 1GB...
 2GB...
```

Performance Tuning

```
3GB...
4GB...
5GB...
6GB...
7GB...
8GB...
9GB...
testing...
options:{ recSizeKB: 8, nThreads: 12, fileSizeMB: 10000, r: true,
mmf: true }
wthr 12
new thread, total running : 1
read:1 write:0
8107 ops/sec
9253 ops/sec
9258 ops/sec
9290 ops/sec
9088 ops/sec
<---- output truncated --->
new thread, total running : 12
read:1 write:0
read:1 write:0
read:1 write:0
read:1 write:0
9430 ops/sec
9668 ops/sec
9804 ops/sec
9619 ops/sec
9371 ops/sec
```

4. Measure the read throughput with mmf enabled and a payload slightly less than the systems total memory:

   ```
   root@ubuntu:~# echo "{ recSizeKB: 8, nThreads: 12, fileSizeMB: 400,
   r: true, mmf: true }" | mongoperf
   ```

   You will see the following:

   ```
   mongoperf
    use -h for help
    parsed options:
    { recSizeKB: 8, nThreads: 12, fileSizeMB: 400, r: true, mmf: true
   }
    creating test file size:400MB ...
    testing...
    options:{ recSizeKB: 8, nThreads: 12, fileSizeMB: 400, r: true,
   mmf: true }
    wthr 12
   ```

Performance Tuning

```
             new thread, total running : 1
             read:1 write:0
             2605344 ops/sec
             4918429 ops/sec
             4720891 ops/sec
             4766924 ops/sec
             4693762 ops/sec
             4810953 ops/sec
             4785765 ops/sec
             4839164 ops/sec
             <---- output truncated --->
             new thread, total running : 12
             read:1 write:0
             read:1 write:0
             read:1 write:0
             read:1 write:0
             4835022 ops/sec
             4962848 ops/sec
             4945852 ops/sec
             4945882 ops/sec
             4970441 ops/sec
```

How it works...

The mongoperf utility takes parameters in the form of a JSON file. We can either provide this configuration in the form of a file or simply pipe the configuration to mongoperf's `stdin`. To view the available options of mongoperf simply run `mongoperf -h` and obtain the following:

```
usage:
 mongoperf < myjsonconfigfile
    {
      nThreads:<n>,     // number of threads (default 1)
      fileSizeMB:<n>,   // test file size (default 1MB)
      sleepMicros:<n>,  // pause for sleepMicros/nThreads between each
operation (default 0)
      mmf:<bool>,       // if true do i/o's via memory mapped files (default
false)
      r:<bool>,         // do reads (default false)
      w:<bool>,         // do writes (default false)
      recSizeKB:<n>,    // size of each write (default 4KB)
      syncDelay:<n>     // secs between fsyncs, like --syncdelay in mongod.
(default 0/never)
    }
```

In step 1, we pass a handful of parameters to mongoperf. Let's take a look at them:

- `recSizeKB`: The size of each record that would be written or read from the sample dataset. In our example, we are using an 8 KB record size.
- `nThreads`: The number of concurrent threads performing the (read/write) operations. In our case, it is set to 12.
- `fileSizeMB`: The size of the file to be read or written to. We are setting this to roughly 10 GB
- `r`: By indicating `r:true`, we will only be performing read operations. You can use `w:true` to test write operations or both.
- `mmf`: It is memory mapped file format. Disabling `mmf` causes mongoperf to bypass the file buffer and perform the operation directly on the disk. In order to truly test the underlying physical I/O, we are disabling `mmf` by setting it to false. In the subsequent steps, we will set it to true.

As we fire up the mongoperf utility, mongoperf first tries to create a roughly 10 GB file on the disk. Once created, it starts one thread and slowly ramps up to 12 (`nThreads`). You can clearly see the increase in read operations per second as the number of threads increases. Depending on your disk's capabilities, you should expect to reach the maximum IOPS limit pretty soon. This can be observed, in step 2, by running the `iostat` command and observing the `%util` column. Once it reaches 100%, you can assume that the disk is peaking at its maximum operating limit.

In step 3, we run the same test but this time with `mmf` set to true. Here, we are attempting to test the benefits of memory mapping by not reading the data from memory and reading it from the physical disk instead. However, you can see that the performance is not as high as we would expect. In fact, it is drastically lower than the IOPS achieved when reading from disk. The primary reason is that our working file is 10 GB in size, whereas my VM's memory is only 1 GB. As the entire dataset cannot fit in memory, mongoperf has to routinely seek data from the disk. This is more suboptimal when the reads are random, and this can be observed in the output. In step 4, we confirm our theory by running the test again but this time, with a `fileSize` of 400 MB, which is smaller than the available memory. As you can see, the number of IOPS is drastically higher than the previous run, confirming that it is extremely important that your working dataset fits in your system's memory.

Performance Tuning

So there you have it, a simple way to test your system's IOPS using the mongoperf utility. Although we only tested read operations, I would strongly urge you to test write as well as read/write operations when testing your systems. Additionally, you should also perform `mmf` enabled tests to give you an idea of what would be an adequate sized working set that you can hold on a given server.

Finding slow running queries and operations

In this recipe, we will be looking at how to capture queries that have longer execution times. By identifying slow running queries, you can work towards implementing appropriate database indexes or even consider optimizing the application code.

Getting ready

Assuming that you are already running a MongoDB server, we will be importing a dataset of around 100,000 records that are available in the form of a CSV file called `chapter_2_mock_data.csv`. You can download this file from the Packt website.

How to do it...

1. Import the sample data into the MongoDB server:

    ```
    mongoimport --headerline --ignoreBlanks --type=csv -d mydb -c mockdata -h localhost chapter_2_mock_data.csv
    ```

    This will give us the following result:

    ```
    2017-06-23T08:12:02.122+0530 connected to: localhost
    2017-06-23T08:12:03.144+0530 imported 100000 documents
    ```

2. Connect to the MongoDB instance and open a MongoDB shell:

    ```
    mongo localhost
    ```

3. Check that the documents are in the right place:

   ```
   > use mydb
   switched to db mydb
   > db.mockdata.count()
   100000
   ```

4. Enable profiling for slow queries:

   ```
   > db.setProfilingLevel(1, 20)
   { "was" : 0, "slowms" : 20, "ok" : 1 }
   ```

5. Run a simple `find` query as follows:

   ```
   > db.mockdata.find({first_name: "Pam"}).count()
   10
   ```

6. Check the profiling collection:

   ```
   > db.system.profile.find().pretty()
   ```

   The following result is obtained:

   ```
   {
       "op" : "command",
       "ns" : "mydb.mockdata",
       "command" : {
           "count" : "mockdata",
           "query" : {
               "first_name" : "Pam"
           },
           "fields" : {

           }
       },
       "keysExamined" : 0,
       "docsExamined" : 100000,
       "numYield" : 781,
       "locks" : {
           "Global" : {
               "acquireCount" : {
                   "r" : NumberLong(1564)
               }
           },
           "Database" : {
               "acquireCount" : {
                   "r" : NumberLong(782)
               }
   ```

```
                },
                "Collection" : {
                    "acquireCount" : {
                        "r" : NumberLong(782)
                    }
                }
            },
            "responseLength" : 29,
            "protocol" : "op_command",
            "millis" : 37,
            "planSummary" : "COLLSCAN",
            "execStats" : {
                "stage" : "COUNT",
                "nReturned" : 0,
                "executionTimeMillisEstimate" : 26,
                "works" : 100002,
                "advanced" : 0,
                "needTime" : 100001,
                "needYield" : 0,
                "saveState" : 781,
                "restoreState" : 781,
                "isEOF" : 1,
                "invalidates" : 0,
                "nCounted" : 10,
                "nSkipped" : 0,
                "inputStage" : {
                    "stage" : "COLLSCAN",
                    "filter" : {
                        "first_name" : {
                            "$eq" : "Pam"
                        }
                    },
                    "nReturned" : 10,
                    "executionTimeMillisEstimate" : 26,
                    "works" : 100002,
                    "advanced" : 10,
                    "needTime" : 99991,
                    "needYield" : 0,
                    "saveState" : 781,
                    "restoreState" : 781,
                    "isEOF" : 1,
                    "invalidates" : 0,
                    "direction" : "forward",
                    "docsExamined" : 100000
                }
            },
            "ts" : ISODate("2017-07-07T03:26:57.818Z"),
            "client" : "192.168.200.1",
```

```
            "appName" : "MongoDB Shell",
            "allUsers" : [ ],
            "user" : ""
    }
```

How it works...

We begin by importing a fairly large dataset using the `mongoimport` utility, as we did in the *Working with indexes* recipe in Chapter 2, *Understanding and Managing Indexes*. Next, in steps 2 and step 3, we start the MongoDB shell and check that our documents were inserted.

In step 4, we enable database profiling by running the `db.setProfilingLevel(1, 20)` command. Database profiling is a feature available in MongoDB that allows you to log slow queries or operations and profiling information related to the operation. MongoDB allows three profiling levels:

- **Level 0**: Disable database profiling
- **Level 1**: Log slow queries
- **Level 2**: Log slow operations

By default, profiling for all databases is set to level 0. This can be confirmed by running the following command:

```
db.getProfilingStatus()
{ "was" : 0, "slowms" : 100 }
```

The `was` field indicates the current profiling level, whereas the `slowms` field indicates the maximum allowed execution time (in milliseconds) for operations. All operations taking longer than the `slowms` threshold will be recorded by the database profiler. In our recipe, we set the profiling level to 1, indicating that we want the profiling level to record only slow queries, and the second parameter, 20, indicates that any query taking longer than 20 ms should be recorded.

In step 5, we run a simple query to count the number of documents that have `first_name = 'Pam'`. As this is not an indexed collection, the server will have to scan through all documents, which hopefully takes more than 20 ms. Once the profiler's threshold is crossed (in our case, 20 ms), the data is stored in the `system.profile` collection.

Performance Tuning

In step 6, we query the `system.profile` collection to find all operations captured by the profiling database. Each document in this collection captures a lot of information regarding the query. A few of them are as follows:

- `client`: The IP address of the connecting client.
- `appName`: This is a string passed by the MongoDB driver that can help identify the connecting app. It's extremely helpful if you have multiple applications talking to the same database. In our example, this string was `"MongoDB Shell"`, which was set by `mongo-shell`.
- `user`: The authenticated user who ran the operation. This can be empty if no authentication was used.
- `millis`: The time taken, in milliseconds, for the entire operation to finish.
- `command`: The command for the given operation.
- `ns`: The namespace on which the command was run. Its format is `<database>.<collection>`, so in our example it was run on the `mydb` database's `mockdata` collection.

An exhaustive list can be found in MongoDB's official documentation, `https://docs.mongodb.com/manual/reference/database-profiler/`.

Considering the wealth of information collected by the database profiler, it should be very easy not only to debug slow queries but even monitor the collection to alert on patterns (more on this in `Chapter 8`, *Monitoring MongoDB*).

There's more...

If, due to sheer boredom or just curiosity, you happened to inspect the `system.profile` collection, you will note that it is a capped collection with a size of 1 MB:

```
db.system.profile.stats()
```

The result is as follows:

```
{
    "ns" : "mydb.system.profile",
    "size" : 0,
    "count" : 0,
    "numExtents" : 1,
    "storageSize" : 1048576,
    "lastExtentSize" : 1048576,
    "paddingFactor" : 1,
    "paddingFactorNote" : "paddingFactor is unused and unmaintained in
```

```
        3.0. It remains hard coded to 1.0 for compatibility only.",
                "userFlags" : 1,
                "capped" : true,
                "max" : NumberLong("9223372036854775807"),
                "maxSize" : 1048576,
                "nindexes" : 0,
                "totalIndexSize" : 0,
                "indexSizes" : {
                },
                "ok" : 1
        }
```

This size may be sufficient for most cases, but if you need to increase the size of this collection, here is how to do it.

First, we disable profiling:

```
> db.setProfilingLevel(0)
{ "was" : 1, "slowms" : 100, "ok" : 1 }
```

Next, we drop the `system.profile` collection and create a new capped collection with a size of 10 MB:

```
> db.createCollection('system.profile', {capped: true, size: 10485760})
{ "ok" : 1 }
```

Finally, enable profiling:

```
> db.setProfilingLevel(1,20)
{ "was" : 0, "slowms" : 100, "ok" : 1 }
```

That's it! Your `system.profile` collection's size is now 10 MB.

Storage considerations when using Amazon EC2

Amazon Web Services (**AWS**) provides a variety of instances in their **Elastic Compute Cloud** (**EC2**) offerings. With each type of EC2 instance, there are two distinct ways to store data: instance store and **Elastic Block Storage** (**EBS**).

Performance Tuning

Instance store refers to an ephemeral disk that is available as a block device to the instance and is physically present on the host of the instance. By being available on the same host, these disks provide extremely high throughput. However, instance stores are ephemeral and thus provide no guarantees of data retention if an instance is terminated, stopped, or the disk fails. This is clearly not suitable for a single node MongoDB instance, as you might lose your data any time the instance goes down. Not all hope is lost, though. We can use a three or more node replica set and ensure the redundancy of data. For a more robust deployment, we can consider having an extra node in the replica set cluster that uses EBS and has a priority set to zero. This ensures that the node is always in sync with the data and at the same time is not used for serving actual queries.

EBS is network-attached storage that can be used as a block device and can be attached to any AWS instance. EBS volumes provide data persistence and can be reattached to any instance running in the same availability zone of the AWS region. There are various forms of EBS volume available, such as standard general purpose SSDs, **Provisioned IOPS (PIOPS)**, and high throughput magnetic disks. As magnetic disks are more focused on high-throughput data streams mostly performing sequential reads on large files, they are not appropriate for MongoDB.

General purpose SSDs provide submillisecond latencies with a minimum baseline of 100 IOPS. It also provides the ability to burst up to 10,000 IOPS depending on the volume type and has a rather unique 3 IOPS per GB burst bucket system, and I would rather not go into too much detail. PIOPS is another EBS offering, in that you can choose a minimum guaranteed IOPS and are billed accordingly. For most small to medium sized workloads, general purpose SSDs should do the trick. However, when provisioning EBS volumes, we need to keep in mind the network utilization.

As EBS volumes are accessed over the network, they tend to share the same network link as that of the instance. This may not be ideal for a database, as the application traffic to the instance would then be contending with that of the EBS volumes. AWS does provide EBS optimized EC2 instances that use a different network path so that your instance traffic does not affect your disk throughput.

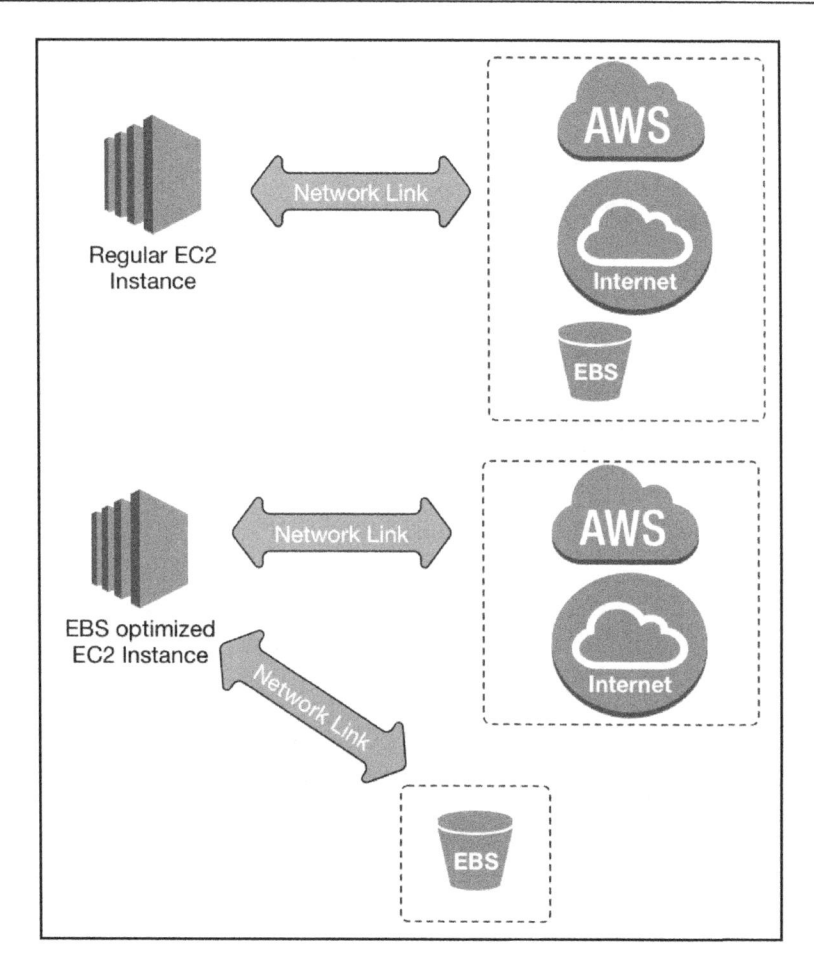

Another significant optimization technique is to use multiple EBS volumes for different parts of your MongoDB data. For instance, we can have separate EBS volumes for the actual data, the database journal, the logs, and the backups. This separation of EBS volumes would ensure that journals, logs, and backup operations do not impinge on the throughput of the actual data.

Lastly, striping volumes over EBS (RAID 0) may prove to increase your overall volume's IOPS capacity. Although the official MongoDB documentation does not recommend using RAID 0 over EBS, I suggest testing your workload against RAID 0 EBS volumes to determine if this suits your needs.

Performance Tuning

More on EBS can be found here: `http://docs.aws.amazon.com/AWSEC2/latest/UserGuide/EBSVolumeTypes.html`.

Figuring out the size of a working set

In this recipe, we will be looking at what a working set is, why is it important, and how to calculate it.

As you probably know, MongoDB relies heavily on caching objects and indexes in RAM. The primary reason to do so is to leverage the speed at which data can be retrieved from RAM as compared to physical disks. Theoretically, a working set is the amount of data accessed by your clients. For performance reasons, it is highly recommended that the server should have sufficient RAM to fit the entire working set while keeping sufficient room for other operations and services running on the same server.

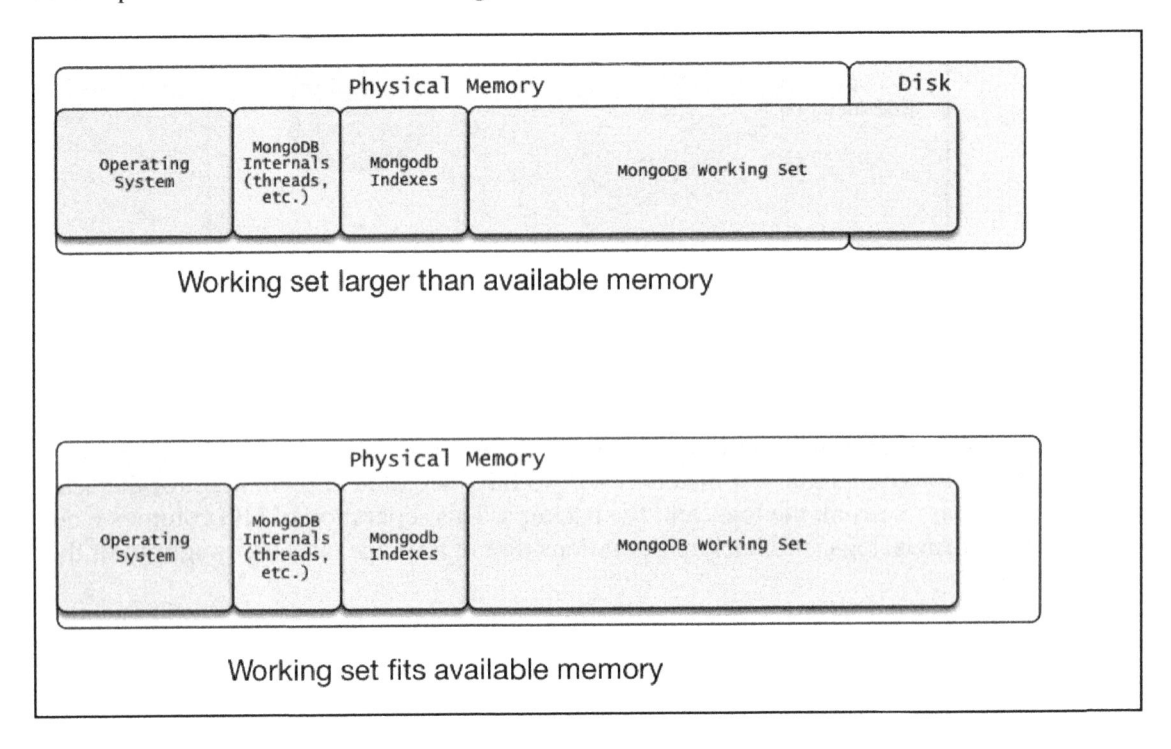

At a high level, the working set comprises the most frequently accessed data and indexes. To get an idea of your database's size, you can run the `db.stats()` command on the MongoDB shell:

```
db.stats()
```

You will get the following result:

```
{
    "db" : "mydb",
    "collections" : 5,
    "views" : 0,
    "objects" : 100009,
    "avgObjSize" : 239.83617474427302,
    "dataSize" : 23985776,
    "storageSize" : 48304128,
    "numExtents" : 12,
    "indexes" : 2,
    "indexSize" : 3270400,
    "fileSize" : 67108864,
    "nsSizeMB" : 16,
    "extentFreeList" : {
        "num" : 1,
        "totalSize" : 1048576
    },
    "dataFileVersion" : {
        "major" : 4,
        "minor" : 22
    },
    "ok" : 1
}
```

In the output, `dataSize` represents the size of entire (uncompressed) data, of the given database and `indexSize` represents the total size of all indexes in the database. In theory, we want to have enough RAM to fit all the data and indexes. This would result in the fewest seeks from the physical storage and provide an optimal read performance. However, for all practical purposes, this scenario may not be true in all cases. Say, for example, you have 24 GB of data and about 2 GB of indexes; it is recommended that you go with a server that has 32 GB RAM. But what if your application usage is such that you barely access about 4 GB of data? In this case, having an over provisioned server may not be an ideal choice. Similarly, if you have a smaller working set, say 6 GB, and you host it on an server with 8 GB RAM, if the rate at which the working set increases is considerably fast, you may soon run out of memory to fit the working set. My point is, while understanding the size of a working set is an absolutely must, you should not underestimate the importance of monitoring the actual usage of the data.

> MongoDB maintains a thread per connection that consumes 1 MB of RAM. Make sure you factor this in when doing capacity planning for your database server.

There's more...

From version 3.0, MongoDB has provided detailed statistics of the WiredTiger storage engine, especially the cache. Here is the output of a production system that has 16 GB of memory. The approximate size of the working set is 600 MB and the index size is 3 MB:

```
> db.serverStatus().wiredTiger.cache
{
   "tracked dirty bytes in the cache" : 0,
   "tracked bytes belonging to internal pages in the cache" : 299485,
   "bytes currently in the cache" : 641133907,
   "tracked bytes belonging to leaf pages in the cache" : 7515893283,
   "maximum bytes configured" : 7516192768,
   "tracked bytes belonging to overflow pages in the cache" : 0,
   "bytes read into cache" : 583725713,
   "bytes written from cache" : 711362477,
<-- output truncated -->
   "tracked dirty pages in the cache" : 0,
   "pages currently held in the cache" : 3674,
    "pages read into cache" : 3784,
    "pages written from cache" : 117710
}
```

By default, WiredTiger uses 50% of RAM (minus 1 GB) or 256 MB for its internal cache. In the preceding output, this can be seen in the value of `maximum bytes configured`, which is roughly 7 GB on a 16 GB RAM server. This parameter can be changed by setting the `wiredTiger.engineConfig.cacheSizeGB` parameter in the MongoDB configuration file, or by setting `wiredTigerEngineRuntimeConfig`.

You should keep an eye on `tracked dirty bytes in the cache`. If this increases consistently to a high number, you may need to look at changing the cache size. Here's a simple rule of thumb:

```
tracked dirty bytes in the cache < bytes currently in the cache < maximum bytes configured
```

4
High Availability with Replication

In this chapter, we will cover the following topics:

- Initializing a new replica set
- Adding a node to the replica set
- Removing a node from the replica set
- Working with an arbiter
- Switching between primary and secondary nodes
- Changing replica set configuration
- Changing priority to replica set nodes

Introduction

This chapter aims to get you started with MongoDB replica sets. A replica set is essentially a group of MongoDB servers that form a quorum and replicate data across all nodes. Such a setup not only provides a high availability cluster but also allows the distribution of database reads across multiple nodes. A replica consists of a single primary node along with secondary nodes.

The primary node accepts all writes to the database, and each write operation is replicated to the secondary nodes through replication of operation logs, which are also known as oplogs.

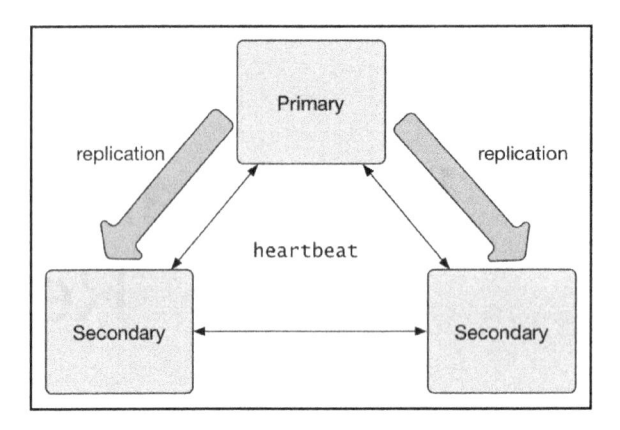

A node is determined as primary by way of an election between the nodes in the replica set. Thus, any node within the cluster can become a primary node at any point. It is important to have an odd number of nodes in the replica set to ensure that the election process does not result in a tie. If you choose to have an even number of nodes in the replica set, MongoDB provides a non-resource intensive arbiter server that can perform heartbeats and take part in the election process.

In this chapter, we will be looking at various aspects of setting up and managing replica sets.

Initializing a new replica set

In this recipe, we will be setting up the first node of a three node replica set on a single server. In a production setup, this should be on three physically separate servers.

Getting ready

By now, I am assuming you are familiar with installing MongoDB and have it ready. Additionally, we will create individual directories for each MongoDB instance:

```
mkdir -p /data/server{1,2,3}/{conf,logs,db}
```

This should create three parent directories: `/data/server1`, `/data/server2`, and `/data/server3`, each containing subdirectories named `conf`, `logs`, and `db`. We will be using this directory format throughout the chapter.

How to do it...

1. Start the first node in the replica set:

   ```
   mongod --dbpath /data/server1/db --replSet MyReplicaSet
   ```

2. Open a new Terminal window, connect to the replica set node using the MongoDB shell, and check the replica set's status:

   ```
   rs.status()
   {
     "info" : "run rs.initiate(...) if not yet done for the set",
     "ok" : 0,
     "errmsg" : "no replset config has been received",
     "code" : 94,
     "codeName" : "NotYetInitialized"
   }
   ```

3. Initialize the replica set:

   ```
   rs.initiate()
   {
      "info2" : "no configuration specified. Using a default configuration for the set",
      "me" : "vagrant-ubuntu-trusty-64:27017",
      "ok" : 1
   }
   ```

4. Check the replica set's status again:

   ```
   rs.status()
   {
    "set" : "MyReplicaSet",
    "date" : ISODate("2017-08-20T05:28:26.827Z"),
    "myState" : 1,
    "term" : NumberLong(1),
    "heartbeatIntervalMillis" : NumberLong(2000),
    "optimes" : {
    "lastCommittedOpTime" : {
    "ts" : Timestamp(1503206903, 1),
    "t" : NumberLong(1)
   ```

```
        },
        "appliedOpTime" : {
            "ts" : Timestamp(1503206903, 1),
            "t" : NumberLong(1)
        },
        "durableOpTime" : {
            "ts" : Timestamp(1503206903, 1),
            "t" : NumberLong(1)
        }
    },
    "members" : [
        {
            "_id" : 0,
            "name" : "vagrant-ubuntu-trusty-64:27017",
            "health" : 1,
            "state" : 1,
            "stateStr" : "PRIMARY",
            "uptime" : 35,
            "optime" : {
                "ts" : Timestamp(1503206903, 1),
                "t" : NumberLong(1)
            },
            "optimeDate" : ISODate("2017-08-20T05:28:23Z"),
            "infoMessage" : "could not find member to sync from",
            "electionTime" : Timestamp(1503206902, 2),
            "electionDate" : ISODate("2017-08-20T05:28:22Z"),
            "configVersion" : 1,
            "self" : true
        }
    ],
    "ok" : 1
}
```

5. Switch back to the mongod Terminal window and inspect the server logs:

```
2017-08-20T05:28:16.928+0000 I NETWORK [thread1] connection
accepted from 192.168.200.1:55765 #1 (1 connection now open)
 2017-08-20T05:28:16.929+0000 I NETWORK [conn1] received client
metadata from 192.168.200.1:55765 conn1: { application: { name:
"MongoDB Shell" }, driver: { name: "MongoDB Internal Client",
version: "3.4.4" }, os: { type: "Darwin", name: "Mac OS X",
architecture: "x86_64", version: "14.5.0" } }
 2017-08-20T05:28:22.625+0000 I COMMAND [conn1] initiate : no
configuration specified. Using a default configuration for the set
 2017-08-20T05:28:22.625+0000 I COMMAND [conn1] created this
configuration for initiation : { _id: "MyReplicaSet", version: 1,
members: [ { _id: 0, host: "vagrant-ubuntu-trusty-64:27017" } ] }
 2017-08-20T05:28:22.625+0000 I REPL [conn1] replSetInitiate admin
```

command received from client
2017-08-20T05:28:22.625+0000 I REPL [conn1] replSetInitiate config object with 1 members parses ok
2017-08-20T05:28:22.625+0000 I REPL [conn1] ******
2017-08-20T05:28:22.625+0000 I REPL [conn1] creating replication oplog of size: 1628MB...
2017-08-20T05:28:22.628+0000 I STORAGE [conn1] Starting WiredTigerRecordStoreThread local.oplog.rs
2017-08-20T05:28:22.628+0000 I STORAGE [conn1] The size storer reports that the oplog contains 0 records totaling to 0 bytes
2017-08-20T05:28:22.628+0000 I STORAGE [conn1] Scanning the oplog to determine where to place markers for truncation
2017-08-20T05:28:22.634+0000 I REPL [conn1] ******
2017-08-20T05:28:22.646+0000 I INDEX [conn1] build index on: admin.system.version properties: { v: 2, key: { version: 1 }, name: "incompatible_with_version_32", ns: "admin.system.version" }
2017-08-20T05:28:22.646+0000 I INDEX [conn1] building index using bulk method; build may temporarily use up to 500 megabytes of RAM
2017-08-20T05:28:22.646+0000 I INDEX [conn1] build index done. scanned 0 total records. 0 secs
2017-08-20T05:28:22.646+0000 I COMMAND [conn1] setting featureCompatibilityVersion to 3.4
2017-08-20T05:28:22.647+0000 I REPL [conn1] New replica set config in use: { _id: "MyReplicaSet", version: 1, protocolVersion: 1, members: [{ _id: 0, host: "vagrant-ubuntu-trusty-64:27017", arbiterOnly: false, buildIndexes: true, hidden: false, priority: 1.0, tags: {}, slaveDelay: 0, votes: 1 }], settings: { chainingAllowed: true, heartbeatIntervalMillis: 2000, heartbeatTimeoutSecs: 10, electionTimeoutMillis: 10000, catchUpTimeoutMillis: 60000, getLastErrorModes: {}, getLastErrorDefaults: { w: 1, wtimeout: 0 }, replicaSetId: ObjectId('59991df64db063a571ae8680') } }
2017-08-20T05:28:22.647+0000 I REPL [conn1] This node is vagrant-ubuntu-trusty-64:27017 in the config
2017-08-20T05:28:22.647+0000 I REPL [conn1] transition to STARTUP2
2017-08-20T05:28:22.647+0000 I REPL [conn1] Starting replication storage threads
2017-08-20T05:28:22.647+0000 I REPL [conn1] Starting replication fetcher thread
2017-08-20T05:28:22.647+0000 I REPL [conn1] Starting replication applier thread
2017-08-20T05:28:22.647+0000 I REPL [conn1] Starting replication reporter thread
2017-08-20T05:28:22.647+0000 I REPL [rsSync] transition to RECOVERING
2017-08-20T05:28:22.648+0000 I REPL [rsSync] transition to SECONDARY
2017-08-20T05:28:22.648+0000 I REPL [rsSync] conducting a dry run

High Availability with Replication

```
    election to see if we could be elected
     2017-08-20T05:28:22.648+0000 I REPL [ReplicationExecutor] dry
    election run succeeded, running for election
     2017-08-20T05:28:22.654+0000 I REPL [ReplicationExecutor] election
    succeeded, assuming primary role in term 1
     2017-08-20T05:28:22.654+0000 I REPL [ReplicationExecutor]
    transition to PRIMARY
     2017-08-20T05:28:22.654+0000 I REPL [ReplicationExecutor] Entering
    primary catch-up mode.
     2017-08-20T05:28:22.654+0000 I REPL [ReplicationExecutor] Exited
    primary catch-up mode.
     2017-08-20T05:28:23.649+0000 I REPL [rsSync] transition to primary
    complete; database writes are now permitted
```

How it works...

In step 1, we begin by starting the mongod process with the two parameters. First, we provide the database path with --dbpath, which is quite standard with all mongod processes. Next, we provide the --replSet parameter with the value MyReplicaSet. This parameter starts the mongod process with the explicit instruction that it will be running a replica set node and the unique name for this replica set is MyReplicaSet. MongoDB uses naming constructs to identify a replica set cluster. This can be changed in the future but would require you to shut down all the nodes within the cluster.

In step 2, we open a different Terminal window and start the mongo shell that is connected to our aforementioned node. We check the replica set's status by running the rs.status() command. If you ever happen to work with replica sets, rs.status() will become the most frequent command you will use for eons to come. I would also like to point out that all major replica set operations are available in the rs.<command> format. To view your options, type rs. (with the trailing dot) and press the *Tab* key twice.

OK, coming back to the output of rs.status(), we can see that MongoDB is indicating that our replica set has not been initialized. We do so by running the rs.initiate() command in step 3. At this point, if you keep pressing the *Enter* key (without any parameters), you can see your mongo shell show the transition of starting the node as a SECONDARY and then PRIMARY:

```
    rs.initiate()
    {
     "info2" : "no configuration specified. Using a default configuration for
    the set",
     "me" : "vagrant-ubuntu-trusty-64:27017",
     "ok" : 1
```

```
}
MyReplicaSet:SECONDARY>
MyReplicaSet:PRIMARY>
MyReplicaSet:PRIMARY>
```

From now on, every time you connect to this node, you will see the replica set name followed by the node's status. Next, we run the `rs.status()` command again and this time get the detailed status of the replica set's configuration. Let's go through some of the key values of the output:

- `set`: This indicates the name of the replica set.
- `myState`: This indicates the status of the current node in the replica set. The most common states you will encounter are as follows:

State number	State	Decription
0	STARTUP	The node is parsing configuration and is starting up
1	PRIMARY	The node is the primary member of the cluster
2	SECONDARY	The node is a secondary member of the cluster
3	RECOVERING	The node is completing either rollback or resync after starting up
7	ARBITER	The node is an arbiter, it does not store any data
8	DOWN	The node is marked as DOWN usually when it is unreachable
10	REMOVED	The node has been removed from the replica set configuration

> There are more MongoDB replica set states; they can be found at https://docs.mongodb.com/manual/reference/replica-states/.

- `heartbeatIntervalMillis`: This indicates the frequency of health checks between nodes in milliseconds.
- `members`: An array containing a list of members currently in the replica set. Each member entry is accompanied by details about the member, such as its name, state, up time, and an information message showing its current state. We will be looking at them more closely in future recipes in this chapter. For now, I just want you to get acquainted with this format.

High Availability with Replication

Once we execute the `rs.initiate()` command, MongoDB attempts to figure out any configuration parameters associated with this replica set (in the form of a config file or mongod command-line flags) and initialized the replica set. In our case, we only mentioned the name of the replica set `MyReplicaSet` as a mongod parameter.

In step 5, by looking at the mongod process logs, we can observe the various stages the application goes through, while trying to bring up a node in a replica set. The information is pretty verbose, so I will not go into detail.

Adding a node to the replica set

In this recipe, we will be looking at how to add a node to an existing replica set.

Getting ready

Ensure that you have a single node replica set running as mentioned in the first recipe of this chapter.

How to do it...

1. Assuming you have the node from the previous recipe already running, open a new Terminal and start a new replica set node:

   ```
   mongod --dbpath /data/server2/db --replSet MyReplicaSet --port 27018
   ```

2. In another Terminal window, connect to the primary server using mongo shell (replace the IP with that of your server's):

   ```
   mongo mongodb://192.168.200.200:27017
   ```

3. Check the number of members in the replica set:

   ```
   rs.status()['members']
   [
   {
   "_id" : 0,
   "name" : "vagrant-ubuntu-trusty-64:27017",
   "health" : 1,
   "state" : 1,
   ```

High Availability with Replication

```
"stateStr" : "PRIMARY",
"uptime" : 36,
"optime" : {
"ts" : Timestamp(1503664489, 1),
"t" : NumberLong(3)
},
"optimeDate" : ISODate("2017-08-25T12:34:49Z"),
"infoMessage" : "could not find member to sync from",
"electionTime" : Timestamp(1503664458, 1),
"electionDate" : ISODate("2017-08-25T12:34:18Z"),
"configVersion" : 1,
"self" : true
}
]
```

4. Add the new node to the replica set:

   ```
   rs.add('192.168.200.200:27018')
   ```

5. Once again, check the members in the replica set:

   ```
   {           "_id" : 0,
       "name" : "vagrant-ubuntu-trusty-64:27017",
       "health" : 1,
       "state" : 1,
       "stateStr" : "PRIMARY",
       "uptime" : 71,
       "optime" : {
           "ts" : Timestamp(1503664527, 1),
           "t" : NumberLong(3)
       },
       "optimeDate" : ISODate("2017-08-25T12:35:27Z"),
       "infoMessage" : "could not find member to sync from",
       "electionTime" : Timestamp(1503664458, 1),
       "electionDate" : ISODate("2017-08-25T12:34:18Z"),
        "configVersion" : 2,
       "self" : true
   },
   {
       "_id" : 1,
       "name" : "192.168.200.200:27018",
       "health" : 1,
       "state" : 0,
       "stateStr" : "STARTUP",
       "uptime" : 1,
       "optime" : {
           "ts" : Timestamp(0, 0),
           "t" : NumberLong(-1)
   ```

High Availability with Replication

```
        },
        "optimeDurable" : {
            "ts" : Timestamp(0, 0),
            "t" : NumberLong(-1)
        },
        "optimeDate" : ISODate("1970-01-01T00:00:00Z"),
        "optimeDurableDate" : ISODate("1970-01-01T00:00:00Z"),
        "lastHeartbeat" : ISODate("2017-08- 5T12:35:27.327Z"),
        "lastHeartbeatRecv" : ISODate("2017-08-5T12:35:27.378Z"),
        "pingMs" : NumberLong(0),
        "configVersion" : -2
}
```

How it works...

As mentioned earlier, this recipe assumes that you are already running the first (primary) node in your replica set, as show in the previous recipe. In step 1, we start another instance of mongod listening on a different port (`27018`). I just want to reiterate that as this is a test setup we will be running all instances of mongod on the same server, but in a production setup all replica set members should be running on separate servers.

In step 2, we look at the output of the `rs.status()` command, more importantly the `members` array. As of now, although we have started a new instance, the primary replica set node is not aware of its existence. Therefore, the list of members would only show one member. Let's fix this.

In step 3, we run `rs.add('192.168.200.200:27018')` in the mongo shell, which is connected to the primary node. The `rs.add()` method is a wrapper around the actual `replSetReconfig` command in that it adds a node to the `members` array and reconfigures the replica set. We will look into replica set reconfiguration in future recipes. Next, we look again at the output of the `rs.status()` command. If you inspect the `members` array, you will find our second member. If you have run the command soon after `rs.add(...)`, you may be able to see the following:

```
    "_id" : 1,
    "name" : "192.168.200.200:27018",
    "health" : 1,
    "state" : 0,
    "stateStr" : "STARTUP",
```

The `"state" : 0` string indicates that the member is parsing its configuration and starting up. If you run the `rs.status()` command again, this should change to `"state" : 2`, indicating that the node is a secondary node.

> 💡 **TIP**
> Keep an eye on the `configVersion` key of each member. Every change in the replica set's configuration increments the value of `configVersion` by one. This can be handy for a members's current configuration state.

To finish off this recipe, I would like you to start another instance of mongod on port `27019` and add it to the cluster.

Removing a node from the replica set

In this recipe, we will be looking at how to remove a member from a replica set. If you have done the previous two recipes in this chapter, this should be a breeze.

Getting ready

For this recipe, we will need a three node replica set. If you don't have one ready, I suggest referring to the first two recipes of this chapter.

How to do it...

1. Open the mongo shell and log in to one of the nodes. Run `rs.status()` to find the primary node:

```
rs.status()['members']
[
    {
        "_id" : 0,
        "name" : "vagrant-ubuntu-trusty-64:27017",
        "health" : 1,
        "state" : 1,
        "stateStr" : "PRIMARY",
        "uptime" : 57933,
        "optime" : {
            "ts" : Timestamp(1503722389, 1),
            "t" : NumberLong(5)
        },
        "optimeDate" : ISODate("2017-08-26T04:39:49Z"),
        "electionTime" : Timestamp(1503721808, 1),
        "electionDate" : ISODate("2017-08-26T04:30:08Z"),
        "configVersion" : 3,
```

High Availability with Replication

```
                "self" : true
            },
            {
                "_id" : 1,
                "name" : "192.168.200.200:27018",
                "health" : 1,
                "state" : 2,
                "stateStr" : "SECONDARY",
                "uptime" : 51609,
                "optime" : {
                    "ts" : Timestamp(1503722389, 1),
                    "t" : NumberLong(5)
                },
                "optimeDurable" : {
                    "ts" : Timestamp(1503722389, 1),
                    "t" : NumberLong(5)
                },
                "optimeDate" : ISODate("2017-08-26T04:39:49Z"),
                "optimeDurableDate" : ISODate("2017-08-26T04:39:49Z"),
                "lastHeartbeat" : ISODate("2017-08-26T04:39:51.239Z"),
                "lastHeartbeatRecv" : ISODate("2017-08-
        6T04:39:51.240Z"),
                "pingMs" : NumberLong(0),
                "syncingTo" : "vagrant-ubuntu-trusty-64:27017",
                "configVersion" : 3
            },
            {
                "_id" : 2,
                "name" : "192.168.200.200:27019",
                "health" : 1,
                "state" : 2,
                "stateStr" : "SECONDARY",
                "uptime" : 84,
                "optime" : {
                    "ts" : Timestamp(1503722389, 1),
                    "t" : NumberLong(5)
                },
                "optimeDurable" : {
                    "ts" : Timestamp(1503722389, 1),
                    "t" : NumberLong(5)
                },
                "optimeDate" : ISODate("2017-08-26T04:39:49Z"),
                "optimeDurableDate" : ISODate("2017-08-26T04:39:49Z"),
                "lastHeartbeat" : ISODate("2017-08-26T04:39:51.240Z"),
                "lastHeartbeatRecv" : ISODate("2017-08-
        6T04:39:51.307Z"),
                "pingMs" : NumberLong(0),
                "syncingTo" : "192.168.200.200:27018",
```

```
                "configVersion" : 3
        }
]
```

2. Run `rs.remove()` to remove the last node in the replica set:

   ```
   rs.remove('192.168.200.200:27019')
   ```

3. Check the status of the replica set:

   ```
   rs.status()['members']
   [
        {
            "_id" : 0,
            "name" : "vagrant-ubuntu-trusty-64:27017",
            "health" : 1,
            "state" : 1,
            "stateStr" : "PRIMARY",
            "uptime" : 57998,
            "optime" : {
                "ts" : Timestamp(1503722449, 2),
                "t" : NumberLong(5)
            },
            "optimeDate" : ISODate("2017-08-26T04:40:49Z"),
            "electionTime" : Timestamp(1503721808, 1),
            "electionDate" : ISODate("2017-08-26T04:30:08Z"),
            "configVersion" : 4,
            "self" : true
        },
        {
            "_id" : 1,
            "name" : "192.168.200.200:27018",
            "health" : 1,
            "state" : 2,
            "stateStr" : "SECONDARY",
            "uptime" : 51673,
            "optime" : {
                "ts" : Timestamp(1503722449, 2),
                "t" : NumberLong(5)
            },
            "optimeDurable" : {
                "ts" : Timestamp(1503722449, 2),
                "t" : NumberLong(5)
            },
            "optimeDate" : ISODate("2017-08-26T04:40:49Z"),
            "optimeDurableDate" : ISODate("2017-08-26T04:40:49Z"),
            "lastHeartbeat" : ISODate("2017-08-26T04:40:55.956Z"),
            "lastHeartbeatRecv" : ISODate("2017-08-
   ```

High Availability with Replication

```
    6T04:40:55.956Z"),
        "pingMs" : NumberLong(0),
        "syncingTo" : "vagrant-ubuntu-trusty-64:27017",
        "configVersion" : 4
    }
]
```

4. Connect to the third replica set node, which we removed, and check `rs.status()`:

```
rs.status()
{
 "state" : 10,
 "stateStr" : "REMOVED",
 "uptime" : 338,
> "optime" : {
 "ts" : Timestamp(1503722619, 1),
 "t" : NumberLong(5)
 },
 "optimeDate" : ISODate("2017-08-26T04:43:39Z"),
 "ok" : 0,
 "errmsg" : "Our replica set config is invalid or we are not a member of it",
 "code" : 93,
 "codeName" : "InvalidReplicaSetConfig"
 }
 MyReplicaSet:OTHER>
```

How it works...

In step 1, we connect to one of the three replica set members and check the replica set status. We want to ensure two things: one, that the connected node is primary, and that the node that we want to remove is secondary.

> You cannot remove a primary node from the replica set. You need to force it into becoming secondary and then remove it. We will look more closely at how to do this in the *Switching between primary and secondary nodes* recipe in this chapter.

Now that we've determined that we are connected to the primary node, in step 2, we remove one node from the replica set. By using `rs.remove()` with the IP and port of the node, we remove the node from the replica set.

High Availability with Replication

In step 3, we confirm that the node is removed by running `rs.status()` to get the list of configured nodes in the cluster. Finally, in step 4, we connect to the mongo shell of the node that we just removed. As soon as you log in, you can observe that the console prompt shows OTHER instead of PRIMARY or SECONDARY. Also, the `rs.status()` command's output confirms that the node is in state 10 (REMOVED), indicating that this node is no longer in the replica set cluster. At this point, I would also like you to go through the mongod logs of this node and observe the sequence of events that occur when we run `rs.remove()`:

```
2017-08-26T04:40:51.338+0000 I REPL     [ReplicationExecutor] Cannot find
self in new replica set configuration; I must be removed; NodeNotFound: No
host described in new configuration 4 for replica set MyReplicaSet maps to
this node
2017-08-26T04:40:51.339+0000 I REPL     [ReplicationExecutor] New replica
set config in use: { _id: "MyReplicaSet", version: 4, protocolVersion: 1,
members: [ { _id: 0, host: "vagrant-ubuntu-trusty-64:27017", arbiterOnly:
false, buildIndexes: true, hidden: false, priority: 1.0, tags: {},
slaveDelay: 0, votes: 1 }, { _id: 1, host: "192.168.200.200:27018",
arbiterOnly: false, buildIndexes: true, hidden:
false, priority: 1.0, tags: {}, slaveDelay: 0, votes: 1 } ], settings: {
chainingAllowed: true, heartbeatIntervalMillis: 2000, heartbeatTimeoutSecs:
10, electionTimeoutMillis: 10000, catchUpTimeoutMillis: 60000,
getLastErrorModes: {}, getLastErrorDefaults: { w: 1, wtimeout: 0 },
replicaSetId: ObjectId('59991df64db063a571ae8680') } }
2017-08-26T04:40:51.339+0000 I REPL     [ReplicationExecutor] This node is
not a member of the config
2017-08-26T04:40:51.339+0000 I REPL     [ReplicationExecutor] transition to
REMOVED
```

As we ran `rs.remove('192.168.200.200:27019')` on the primary node, a new configuration was generated. This configuration is sent to all new or existing nodes of the replica set and the relevant changes are implemented. In the log output shown previously, you can see that the replica set node got the new configuration and figured out that it had been removed from the replica set cluster. It then reconfigured itself and transitioned to the REMOVED state.

Working with an arbiter

In MongoDB, nodes within replica sets perform elections to select a primary node. To ensure there is always a majority in the number of nodes, you can add an arbiter to the replica set. An arbiter is a mongod instance that does not store data but is only involved in voting during an election process. This can prove very useful, especially during network partitions that result in conflicting votes.

Getting ready

We can continue on from the previous recipe, in that all we need is a two node replica set.

How to do it...

1. Create directories for the arbiter process:

   ```
   mkdir -p /data/arbiter/db
   ```

2. Start the arbiter process:

   ```
   mongod --dbpath /data/arbiter/db --replSet MyReplicaSet --port 30000
   ```

3. Open a new Terminal window and connect to the primary node:

   ```
   mongo mongodb://192.168.200.200:27017
   ```

4. Add the arbiter:

   ```
   rs.addArb('192.168.200.200:30000')
   ```

5. Check the members of the replica set:

   ```
   rs.status()['member']
   [
   {
           "_id" : 0,
           "name" : "vagrant-ubuntu-trusty-64:27017",
           "health" : 1,
           "state" : 1,
           "stateStr" : "PRIMARY",
           "uptime" : 61635,
           "optime" : {
               "ts" : Timestamp(1503726090, 1),
               "t" : NumberLong(8)
           },
           "optimeDate" : ISODate("2017-08-26T05:41:30Z"),
           "electionTime" : Timestamp(1503725438, 1),
           "electionDate" : ISODate("2017-08-26T05:30:38Z"),
           "configVersion" : 5,
           "self" : true
   },
   {
   ```

```
            "_id" : 1,
            "name" : "192.168.200.200:27018",
            "health" : 1,
            "state" : 2,
            "stateStr" : "SECONDARY",
            "uptime" : 1214,
            "optime" : {
                "ts" : Timestamp(1503726090, 1),
                "t" : NumberLong(8)
            },
            "optimeDurable" : {
                "ts" : Timestamp(1503726090, 1),
                "t" : NumberLong(8)
            },
            "optimeDate" : ISODate("2017-08-26T05:41:30Z"),
            "optimeDurableDate" : ISODate("2017-08-26T05:41:30Z"),
            "lastHeartbeat" : ISODate("2017-08-26T05:41:32.024Z"),
            "lastHeartbeatRecv" :
ISODate("2017-08-26T05:41:30.034Z"),
            "pingMs" : NumberLong(0),
            "configVersion" : 5
        },
        {
            "_id" : 2,
            "name" : "192.168.200.200:30000",
            "health" : 1,
            "state" : 7,
            "stateStr" : "ARBITER",
            "uptime" : 3,
            "lastHeartbeat" : ISODate("2017-08-26T05:41:32.025Z"),
            "lastHeartbeatRecv" :
ISODate("2017-08-26T05:41:30.034Z"),
            "pingMs" : NumberLong(0),
            "configVersion" : 5
        }
    ]
```

How it works...

We begin by creating the directories for the arbiter process. As mentioned in the beginning of this recipe, an arbiter is nothing but a mongod process that will not store any data. However, it does need to store some metadata about itself and hence a minimal amount of state has to be maintained.

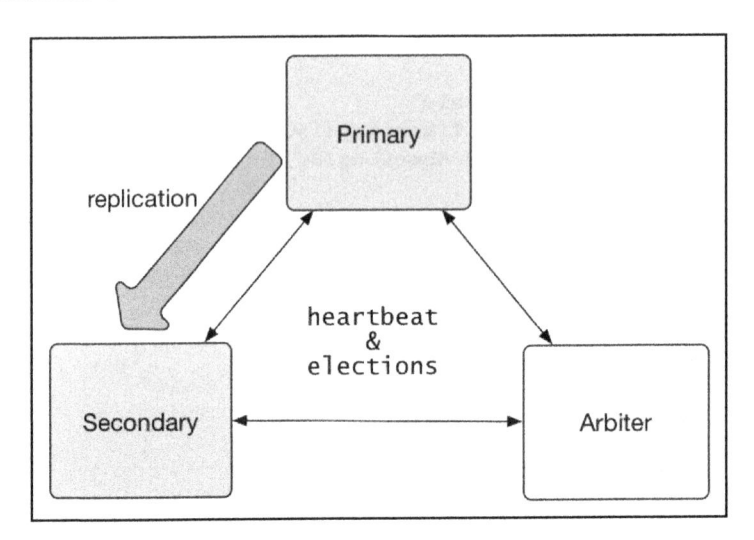

For this purpose, in step 2, we provide the `--dbpath` parameter with a location to store its data along with an arbitrary port 30000.

In step 3, we connect to the primary node of our replica set, and in step 4, we use the `rs.addArb()` wrapper to add the new arbiter.

Next, in step 4, we check the status of the replica set; lo and behold, the mighty arbiter is added to the replica set. If you look at the state and `stateStr` keys, you will see that this member is set `state` to 7, which confirms it is an arbiter.

Switching between primary and secondary nodes

In this recipe, we will be looking at how to force a primary node to become secondary and vice versa. Let's get to it then.

Getting ready

We need a three node replica set, preferably without an arbiter. If you have followed the previous recipes, we should have three mongod instances running on the same instance on three different ports, `27017`, `27018`, and `27019`. In order to keep things simple, we will call them node 1, node 2, and node 3 respectively. Here, we assume that node 1 is primary, whereas node 2 and node 3 are secondary. In the first part of this recipe, we will force node 1 to become secondary. Assuming that node 3 gets elected as primary, in the second part of the recipe, we will try to make node 1 primary.

How to do it...

1. Connect to the primary member (node 1) of the replica set:

   ```
   mongo mongodb://192.168.200.200:27017
   ```

2. Force it to become secondary:

   ```
   rs.stepDown()
   ```

3. Confirm the member is now secondary:

   ```
   rs.isMaster()['ismaster']
   ```

4. Log in to node 2, assuming it is secondary, and prevent it from getting elected:

   ```
   mongo mongodb://192.168.200.200:27018
   rs.freeze(120)
   ```

5. Log in to the newly elected primary node (node 3) of the replica set:

   ```
   mongo mongodb://192.168.200.200:27019
   rs.stepDown()
   ```

6. Force it to become secondary and prevent it from getting elected:

   ```
   rs.freeze(120)
   ```

7. Check that the desired node (node 1) is now primary:

   ```
   mongo mongodb://192.168.200.200:27017
   rs.isMaster()['ismaster']
   ```

How it works...

Forcing a primary node to step down is a fairly straightforward process. As shown in steps 1 and step 2, we just need to log in to the primary node and run the `rs.stepDown()` command. This forces the node to become secondary and initiates an election in the replica set. Within a few seconds (or less), one of the secondary nodes would be elected as the new primary node. In this recipe, we assume that node 3 got elected as the new primary node.

In step 3, we run another neat little helper, `rs.isMaster()`, and look for the value of the `ismaster` key. If its value is set to true, then the current node is a primary. Otherwise, it is a secondary.

For the next part, we work towards converting a particular secondary node to a primary node. This involves a new command called `rs.freeze()`. This wrapper executes the `replSetFreeze` command, which prevents the member from seeking election. So, our strategy is to prevent all nodes from seeking election, except for the one that we want to become the primary.

We do exactly the same in step 4. Here, we log in to node 2 and run `rs.freeze(120)`, which prevents it from seeking election for the next 120 seconds.

Next, in step 5, we log in to our newly elected primary, node 3, and make it step down as primary. Finally, in step 6, we run `rs.freeze(120)`, which prevents it from seeking election for the next 120 seconds.

Once done, we confirm that node 1 is now our primary, as expected. All hail Cthulhu!

Changing replica set configuration

Up until now, we were performing replica set modifications using helper functions like `rs.add()`, `rs.remove()`, and so on. As mentioned earlier, these functions are wrappers which modify the replica set configuration. In this recipe, we will be looking at how to fetch and change the replica set configuration. This can be helpful for various operations like setting priorities, delayed nodes, changing member hostnames, and so on.

Getting ready

For this recipe, you will need a three node replica set.

How to do it...

1. Connect to the primary member of the replica set using the mongo shell:

    ```
    mongo mongodb://192.168.200.200:27017
    ```

2. Fetch the configuration:

    ```
    conf = rs.conf()
    ```

3. Remove the third member of the replica set:

    ```
    conf['members'].pop(2)
    ```

4. Reconfigure the replica set:

    ```
    rs.reconfig(conf)
    ```

5. Confirm that the third node was removed by inspecting the output of rs.status():

    ```
    rs.status()['members']
    ```

6. Add the third node back to the replica set:

    ```
    member = {"_id": 2, "host": "192.168.200.200:27019"}
    conf['members'].push(member)
    ```

7. Reconfigure the replica set:

    ```
    rs.reconfig(conf)
    ```

8. Confirm that the addition was successful:

    ```
    rs.status()['members']
    ```

How it works..

Like our previous recipes, replica set configuration operations can only be performed on the primary node. Once we connect to the primary node, we fetch the running configuration of the replica set using rs.conf(). In step 2, we are storing the value of rs.conf() in a variable called conf. The replica set configuration is a JavaScript object, and therefore we can modify it within the mongo shell.

The configuration contains an array of members. So, in order to remove a member, we simply have to remove its entry from the array and reload the configuration with the new values. In step 3, we use the JavaScript native pop() method to remove an entry from the members array. By running conf['members'].pop(2) we are removing the third entry from the array (note that array indexes start from zero). Next, in step 4, we simply run the rs.reconfig() function while providing it the modified configuration. This function reloads the configuration, and in step 5, we can confirm that the node was indeed removed.

In step 6, we create an object that contains the _id and host entry for the node that we wish to add. Next, we append the configuration's members array and add this entry to it. Finally, in step 7, we reload the configuration again and confirm that the node was added back to the replica set.

Changing priority to replica set nodes

By now, you would have noticed the `priority` keyword in the `rs.status()` output. Replica set members with higher priorities are more likely to be elected as primaries. The value of a priority can range from `0` to `1000`, where `0` indicates a non-voting member. A non-voting member functions as a regular member of a replica set but cannot vote in elections nor get elected as a primary.

Getting ready

For this recipe, we need a three node replica set.

How to do it...

1. Connect to the primary member of the replica set using the mongo shell:

    ```
    mongo mongodb://192.168.200.200:27017
    ```

2. Fetch the configuration:

    ```
    conf = rs.conf()
    ```

3. Change the priorities of all members:

    ```
    conf['members'][0].priority = 5
    conf['members'][1].priority = 2
    conf['members'][2].priority = 2
    ```

4. Reconfigure the replica set:

    ```
    rs.reconfig(conf)
    ```

5. Check the new configuration:

    ```
    rs.conf()['members']
    ```

How it works...

Like our previous recipe, we connect to the primary node and fetch the replica set configuration object. Next, in step 3, we modify the value of the `priority` key of each member in the `members` array. In step 4, we reconfigure the replica set configuration. Lastly, in step 5, we can confirm that the changes have taken effect by inspecting the output of the `rs.conf()` command.

So, why would you need to set priorities in the first place? Well, there can be various circumstances when you would need to have control over which member gets elected as a leader. As a simple example, you need to perform sequential maintenance on your replica set members. You can control which node becomes primary if an election kicks in during the maintenance.

There's more...

Along with priority, we can also set delayed sync and hidden members in replica sets. We will be looking closely at how to set these up later in the book in `Chapter 7`, *Restoring MongoDB from Backups*.

5
High Scalability with Sharding

In this chapter, we will cover the following recipes:

- Setting up and configuring a shard cluster
- Managing chunks
- Moving non-sharded collection data from one shard to another
- Removing a shard from the cluster
- Understanding tag aware sharding – zones

Understanding sharding and its components

In the previous chapter, we saw how MongoDB provides high availability using replica sets. Replica sets also allow distributing read queries across slaves, thus providing a fair bit of load distribution across a cluster of nodes. We have also seen that MongoDB performs most optimally if its working datasets can fit in memory with minimal disk operations. However, as databases grow, it becomes harder to provision servers that can effectively fit the entire working set in memory. This is one of the most common scalability problems faced by most growing organizations.

To address this, MongoDB provides sharding of collections. Sharding allows dividing the data into smaller chunks and distributing it across multiple machines.

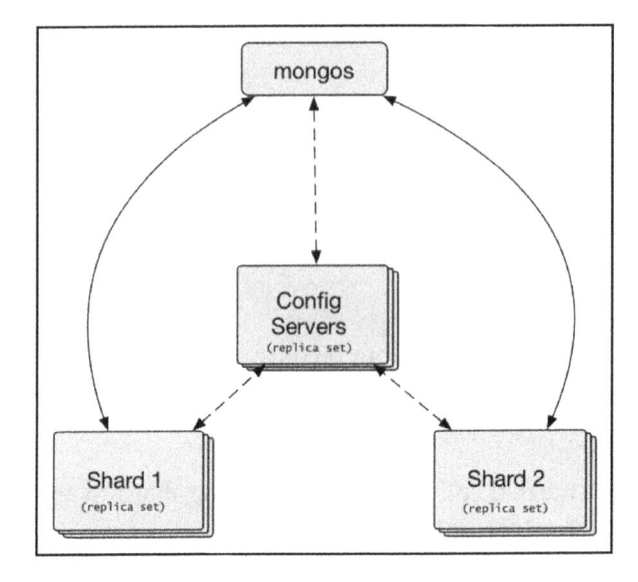

Components of MongoDB sharding infrastructure

Unlike replica sets, a sharded MongoDB cluster consists of multiple components.

Config server

The config server is used to store metadata about the sharded cluster. It contains details about authorizations, as well as admin and config databases. The metadata stored in the config server is read by mongos and shards, making its role extremely important during the operation of the sharded cluster. Thus, it is highly recommended that the config server is setup as a replica set, with appropriate backup and monitoring configured.

The mongos query router

MongoDB's mongos server acts as an interface between the application and the sharded cluster. First, it gathers information (metadata) about the sharded cluster from the config server (described later). Once it has the relevant information about the sharded cluster, it acts as a proxy for all the read and write operations on the cluster. In that, applications only talk to the mongos server and never talks directly to a shard.

More information on how mongos routes queries can be seen at: `https://docs.mongodb.com/manual/core/sharded-cluster-query-router/`.

The shard server

The shard server is nothing but a mongod instance and is executed with the `--shardsvr` switch. The config server delegates chunks to each shard server based on the shard key used for the collection. All queries, executed on the shard, have to originate through the mongos query router. Applications should never directly communicate with a standalone shard.

Choosing the shard key

In order to partition data across multiple shards, MongoDB uses a shard key. This is an immutable key that can be used to identify a document within a sharded collection. Based on boundaries of the shard key, the data is then divided into chunks and spread across multiple shards within a cluster. It is important to note that MongoDB provides sharding at the collection level and a sharded collection can have only one shard key. As shard keys are immutable, we cannot change a key once it is set. It is extremely important to properly plan shard keys before setting up a sharded cluster.

MongoDB provides two sharding strategies—a hashed shard key and ranged shard key.

In hashed shard keys, MongoDB computes and indexes on the hash of the shard key. The data is then evenly distributed across the cluster. So at the expense of a broadcast query, we can achieve even distribution of data across all shards.

A ranged shard key is the default shard key strategy used by MongoDB. In this strategy, MongoDB splits the ranges into chunks and distributes these chunks accordingly. This increases the chance of documents, which have a close proximity to the key value, to be stored on the same shard. In such cases, queries would not be broadcast to all the shards and DB operations would become faster. However, this can also lead to shards getting overloaded on a certain type of keys.

For example, if we do a ranged key on language and keep adding a high number of documents for English speaking users, then the shard holding the key would get all the documents. So there is a good chance that document distribution would be uneven.

So it is extremely important to plan out your sharding strategy far in advance. All aspects of your applications must be thoroughly understood before choosing a shard key strategy.

More information about shard key specifications can be found at: `https://docs.mongodb.com/manual/core/sharding-shard-key`.

Setting up and configuring a sharded cluster

In this recipe, we will look at how to set up a sharded cluster in MongoDB. The cluster includes config servers, shards, and mongos servers. As this is a test setup, we will be running all relevant binaries from a single virtual machine; however, in production, they should be located on separate nodes. Next, we will look at how to enable sharding on a database, followed by sharding an actual collection. Once the sharded cluster is ready, we will import some data to the cluster and execute queries that would give us a glimpse of how the data is partitioned across the shards. Much fun awaits, let's get started!

Getting ready

There are no additional components required besides standard MongoDB binaries. Create the following directories in advance for the config server as well as the shards:

```
mkdir -p /data/{cfgserver1,shard1,shard2,shard3}/data
```

How to do it...

1. Start the config server:

    ```
    mongod --configsvr --dbpath /data/cfgserver1/data --port 27019 --replSet MyConfigRepl
    ```

2. Initialize the config server replica set:

    ```
    mongo localhost:27019
    rs.initiate()

    {
     "info2" : "no configuration specified. Using a default configuration for the set",
     "me" : "vagrant-ubuntu-trusty-64:27019",
     "ok" : 1
    }
    ```

```
rs.status()['configsvr']

true
```

3. Start three shard servers:

   ```
   mongod --shardsvr --dbpath /data/shard1/data --port 27027
   mongod --shardsvr --dbpath /data/shard2/data --port 27028
   mongod --shardsvr --dbpath /data/shard3/data --port 27029
   ```

4. Start the mongos query router:

   ```
   mongos --configdb MyConfigRepl/192.168.200.200:27019
   ```

5. Connect to the mongos server and add the shard mongo `mongodb://127.0.0.1:27017`. Then add the shards to the cluster:

   ```
   sh.addShard('192.168.200.200:27027')

   { "shardAdded" : "shard0000", "ok" : 1 }

   sh.addShard('192.168.200.200:27028')

   { "shardAdded" : "shard0001", "ok" : 1 }

   sh.addShard('192.168.200.200:27029')

   { "shardAdded" : "shard0002", "ok" : 1 }

   sh.status()

   --- Sharding Status ---
    sharding version: {
    "_id" : 1,
    "minCompatibleVersion" : 5,
    "currentVersion" : 6,
    "clusterId" : ObjectId("59c7950c9be3cff24816915a")
    }
    shards:
    { "_id" : "shard0000", "host" : "192.168.200.200:27027", "state" : 1 }
    { "_id" : "shard0001", "host" : "192.168.200.200:27028", "state" : 1 }
    { "_id" : "shard0002", "host" : "192.168.200.200:27029", "state" : 1 }
     <-- output truncated -->
   ```

High Scalability with Sharding

6. Enable sharding for a database:

```
sh.enableSharding('myShardedDB')
{ "ok" : 1 }
sh.status()

--- Sharding Status ---
 <--output truncated-->
 databases:
 { "_id" : "myShardedDB", "primary" : "shard0001", "partitioned" :
true }
```

7. Shard a collection:

```
sh.shardCollection('myShardedDB.people', {language: 1})
{ "collectionsharded" : "myShardedDB.people", "ok" : 1 }

sh.status()

--- Sharding Status ---
 sharding version: {
 "_id" : 1,
 "minCompatibleVersion" : 5,
 "currentVersion" : 6,
 "clusterId" : ObjectId("59c7950c9be3cff24816915a")
 }
 shards:
 { "_id" : "shard0000", "host" : "192.168.200.200:27027", "state" :
1 }
 { "_id" : "shard0001", "host" : "192.168.200.200:27028", "state" :
1 }
 { "_id" : "shard0002", "host" : "192.168.200.200:27029", "state" :
1 }
 <-- output truncated -->
 databases:
 { "_id" : "myShardedDB", "primary" : "shard0001", "partitioned" :
true }
 myShardedDB.people
 shard key: { "language" : 1 }
 unique: false
 balancing: true
 chunks:
 shard0001  1
 { "language" : { "$minKey" : 1 } } -->> { "language" : { "$maxKey"
: 1 } } on : shard0001 Timestamp(1, 0)
```

[112]

8. Add some data to our database:

   ```
   mongoimport -h 192.168.200.200 --type csv --headerline -d
   myShardedDB -c people chapter_2_mock_data.csv
   ```

9. Inspect the data distribution:

   ```
   sh.status()

   --- Sharding Status ---
   --- <output truncated> ---
     { "_id" : "myShardedDB", "primary" : "shard0001", "partitioned" :
   true }
     myShardedDB.people
     shard key: { "language" : 1 }
     unique: false
     balancing: true
     chunks:
     shard0000 1
     shard0001 2
     shard0002 1
     { "language" : { "$minKey" : 1 } } -->> { "language" : "" } on :
   shard0000 Timestamp(2, 0)
     { "language" : "" } -->> { "language" : "Irish Gaelic" } on :
   shard0002 Timestamp(3, 0)
     { "language" : "Irish Gaelic" } -->> { "language" : "Norwegian" }
   on : shard0001 Timestamp(3, 1)
     { "language" : "Norwegian" } -->> { "language" : { "$maxKey" : 1 }
   } on : shard0001 Timestamp(1, 4)
   ```

10. Fetch some records from a single shard:

    ```
    db.people.find({ "language" : "Norwegian" }).explain()

    {
    "queryPlanner" : {
    "mongosPlannerVersion" : 1,
    "winningPlan" : {
    "stage" : "SINGLE_SHARD",
    "shards" : [
    {
    "shardName" : "shard0001",
    "connectionString" : "192.168.200.200:27028",
    <--output truncated -->
    ```

11. Fetch records from multiple shards:

    ```
    db.people.find({ "language": {"$in": ["Norwegian", "Arabic"]}
    }).explain()

    {
     "queryPlanner" : {
     "mongosPlannerVersion" : 1,
     "winningPlan" : {
     "stage" : "SHARD_MERGE",
     "shards" : [
     {
     "shardName" : "shard0001",
     <-- output truncated -->
     "shardName" : "shard0002",
     <-- output truncated -->
    ```

How it works...

We begin setting up the sharded cluster by starting a single instance of the config server in step 1. As of MongoDB 3.4, it is required that the config server is set up as a replica set. However, for demonstration purposes, we are only going to run one config server in this replica set. The service runs through the mongod binary with the `--configsvr` parameter and takes in `--dbpath` as well as `--port`. As the config server contains metadata, including authorization details, it does make sense to run it as a replica set while ensuring we maintain optimal backups and monitoring. We will cover more on the latter in future chapters.

In step 2, we connect to the config server using mongo shell and initiate the replica set. This is a pretty straightforward operation, as we have seen previously in Chapter 2, *Understanding and Managing Indexes*. The only point I've highlighted here is that if you run `rs.status()` on a config server, you should see a key which says `'configsvr' : true`. This key should be verified to confirm that the replica set is indeed for your config server.

In step 3, we start three instances of mongod shards, each pointing to a separate `--dbpath` and `--port`. Up until this point, the shards are not configured, and hence, they are simply waiting for information from the config server.

High Scalability with Sharding

In step 4, we start the mongos service and explicitly point it to the config server replica set using the `--configdb` switch. You will note that the connection string takes the name of the config server replica set as its prefix and is followed by the IP/hostname of the config server; for example,

`ReplicaSetName/host1:port1,host2:port2,...hostN:portN`

At this point, our sharded cluster not contains a config server and a query router (mongos). We now need to add the shard servers to the cluster. To begin, we connect to the mongos service (in step 5) and use the `sh.addShard()` function to add each shard:

```
sh.addShard('192.168.200.200:27027')
{ "shardAdded" : "shard0000", "ok" : 1 }
```

> **TIP**
> All shard management commands have helper functions within the `sh.<function-name>` namespace. For example, `sh.status()`, `sh.addShard()`, and so on.

The string `shard0000` is a unique ID of this shard. By running `sh.status()`, we can confirm that all three shards have been added, each with a unique ID. Additionally, you can also observe that at this point the databases section, in the `sh.status()` output, is empty (this is expected).

In step 6, we enable sharding for the database `myShardedDB` by using the command `sh.enableSharding('myShardedDB')`. If you run the `sh.status()` command, you will observe that the databases section now shows the following:

`{ "_id" : "myShardedDB", "primary" : "shard0001", "partitioned" : true }`

Here, MongoDB has assigned shard with ID `shard001` as the primary shard for the database (chances are that your setup may have chosen a different ID, and that's okay). There is a good chance that you would have more than one collection in your database. Hence, MongoDB selects a primary shard to store data of non-sharded collections.

Now comes the most important part of this whole exercise—selecting the shard key. As shards store data in chunks, distribution of chunks is determined by the type of sharding key used. As discussed in the previous section of this chapter, by default, MongoDB uses ranged keys. We will use this key type in our example setup as well.

In step 7, we shard the collection named `people` on the field `language`. This creates a ranged sharding key on the `language` field in ascending order. Run `sh.status()` and view the databases section in the command output.

[115]

As we have no data in the collection, you should see there is exactly one chunk, on shard0001, and it covers the entire range of the field, that is, from $minKey to $maxKey.

In step 8, we import some sample data in our newly sharded collection. The data imported is available in the file chapter_2_mock_data.csv, which can be downloaded from the Packt website.

Now that we have the data imported, let's have a look at the status of the shard. In step 9, we run sh.status() and inspect the databases section of the output. You can see that, based on the index created in the field language, MongoDB has partitioned the data in four chunks across all three shards. As we have used a ranged shard key, the partitions are performed on string values of the language key. For example, shard0001 has two chunks: one contains all the documents of the language field, ranging from Irish Gaelic to Norwegian, and the other chunk contains all values from Norwegian to $maxKey (end of index).

With this information in mind, we now know that all records for {language: "Norwegian"} would reside on one shard, that is shard0001. This can be confirmed by running a find() operation, as seen in step 10. The winning plan indicates that the result was obtained from a single shard.

In step 11, we run a similar query, but this time the range spreads across multiple shards. In that, mongos would make a query to two shards (shard0001 and shard0002), and await their response. Then, mongos would merge the results and present it to the application (in our case, mongo shell).

As an exercise, I would suggest you re-create the cluster, but with hashed key type, and observe how the chunks are created.

Managing chunks

By now, you should be familiar with the notion of chunks in a MongoDB sharded cluster. In this recipe, we will look at how to split chunks and migrate them across shards.

Getting ready

Ensure you have a sharded cluster ready. If you are reusing the setup from the previous recipe, ensure that you drop the database, as such:

```
use myShardedDB
db.dropDatabase()
```

Before we import the mock data, enable sharding:

```
sh.enableSharding('myShardedDB')
  sh.shardCollection('myShardedDB.users', {age: 1})
```

Finally, we need to import the mock data using the mongoimport utility:

```
mongoimport -h 192.168.200.200 --type csv --headerline -d myShardedDB -c
users chapter_5_mock_data.csv
```

How to do it...

1. Connect to the mongos service and inspect the chunks:

    ```
    sh.status()

    --- Sharding Status ---
     sharding version: {
     <-- output truncated -- >
     databases:
     { "_id" : "myShardedDB", "primary" : "shard0002", "partitioned" :
    true }
     myShardedDB.users
     shard key: { "age" : 1 }
     unique: false
     balancing: true
     chunks:
     shard0000 1
     shard0001 1
     shard0002 2
     { "age" : { "$minKey" : 1 } } -->> { "age" : 18 } on : shard0000
    Timestamp(2, 0)
     { "age" : 18 } -->> { "age" : 54 } on : shard0001 Timestamp(3, 0)
     { "age" : 54 } -->> { "age" : 73 } on : shard0002 Timestamp(3, 1)
     { "age" : 73 } -->> { "age" : { "$maxKey" : 1 } } on : shard0002
    Timestamp(1, 4)
    ```

High Scalability with Sharding

2. Disable the balancer:

   ```
   sh.stopBalancer()
   ```

3. Select the `admin` database and split the chunk:

   ```
   use admin

   db.runCommand({split: 'myShardedDB.users', middle: {age: 50}})
   ```

4. Inspect the chunks again:

   ```
   sh.status()

   --- Sharding Status ---
   <-- output truncated -->
   databases:
   { "_id" : "myShardedDB", "primary" : "shard0002", "partitioned" : true }
   myShardedDB.users
   shard key: { "age" : 1 }
   unique: false
   balancing: true
   chunks:
   shard0000 1
   shard0001 2
   shard0002 2
   { "age" : { "$minKey" : 1 } } -->> { "age" : 18 } on : shard0000 Timestamp(2, 0)
   { "age" : 18 } -->> { "age" : 50 } on : shard0001 Timestamp(3, 2)
   { "age" : 50 } -->> { "age" : 54 } on : shard0001 Timestamp(3, 3)
   { "age" : 54 } -->> { "age" : 73 } on : shard0002 Timestamp(3, 1)
   { "age" : 73 } -->> { "age" : { "$maxKey" : 1 } } on : shard0002 Timestamp(1, 4)
   ```

5. Migrate a chunk from `shard0001` to `shard0000`:

   ```
   sh.moveChunk('myShardedDB.users', {age: 52}, "shard0000")

   { "millis" : 177, "ok" : 1 }
   ```

6. Enable the balancer and inspect the chunks:

```
sh.startBalancer()

{ "ok" : 1 }

sh.status()

--- Sharding Status ---
 <-- output truncated -->
 databases:
 { "_id" : "myShardedDB", "primary" : "shard0002", "partitioned" :
true }
 myShardedDB.users
 shard key: { "age" : 1 }
 unique: false
 balancing: true
 chunks:
 shard0000 2
 shard0001 1
 shard0002 2
 { "age" : { "$minKey" : 1 } } -->> { "age" : 18 } on : shard0000
Timestamp(2, 0)
  { "age" : 18 } -->> { "age" : 50 } on : shard0001 Timestamp(4, 1)
  { "age" : 50 } -->> { "age" : 54 } on : shard0000 Timestamp(4, 0)
  { "age" : 54 } -->> { "age" : 73 } on : shard0002 Timestamp(3, 1)
  { "age" : 73 } -->> { "age" : { "$maxKey" : 1 } } on : shard0002
Timestamp(1, 4)
```

How it works...

For this recipe, we've intentionally used a dataset that can help us work with ranged shard keys. In our mock data, we are going to shard on the age field, as it is always going to be numeric.

In step 1, we connect to the mongos service and inspect the shards and their corresponding chunks. In this example output, you can see that the data is partitioned into four chunks, ranging from $minKey to 18, 18 to 54, 54 to 73, and 73 to $maxKey.

You can also observe that shard0002 has two chunks whereas the other two shards have one chunk each.

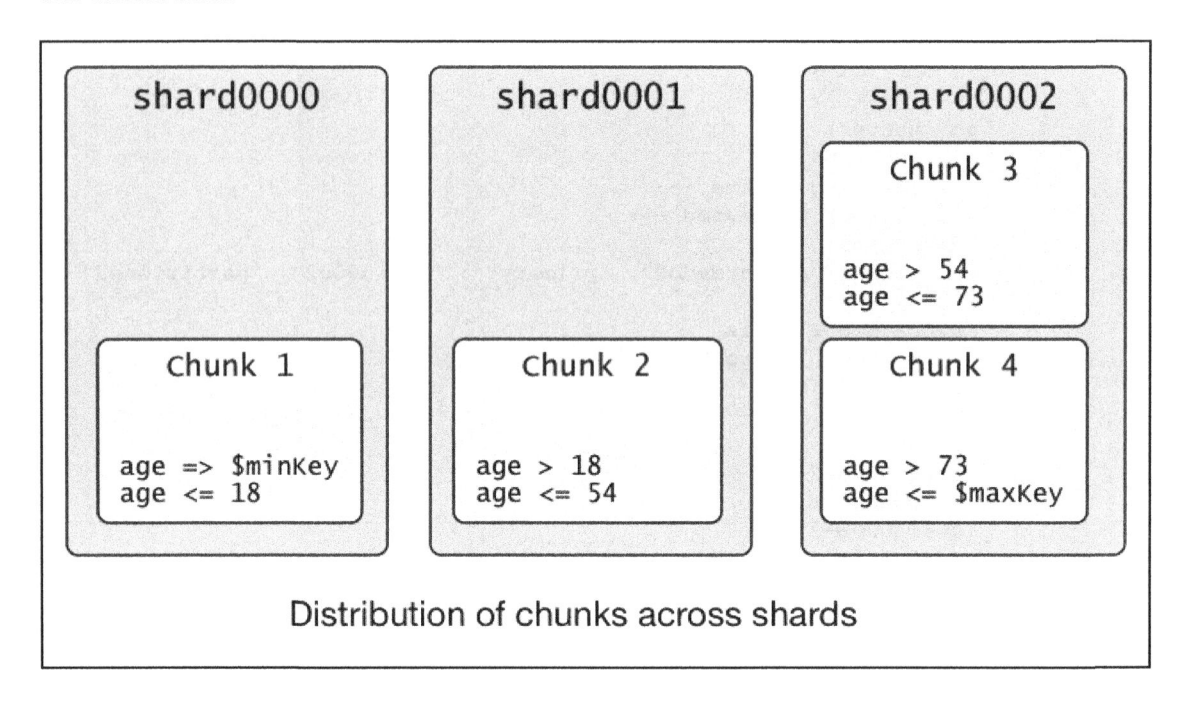

```
shard0000                    shard0001                    shard0002

                                                          Chunk 3

                                                          age > 54
                                                          age <= 73

Chunk 1                      Chunk 2                      Chunk 4

age => $minKey               age > 18                     age > 73
age <= 18                    age <= 54                    age <= $maxKey
```

Distribution of chunks across shards

This distribution of chunks is carried out by MongoDB's balancer service. This is a background process that runs on the config server and performs chunk migrations, ensuring chunks are evenly distributed across the shards. As chunk migration has implications on performance, the balancer ensures that a shard only performs one migration at a time. Additionally, the number of chunks that should be held by a shard is determined by the maximum migration threshold, as described at:
https://docs.mongodb.com/manual/core/sharding-balancer-administration/#sharding-migration-thresholds.

Next, in step 2, we stop the balancer process before we proceed to split the chunks. In step 3, we select the admin database and perform a chunk split on the range, midway to {age: 50}. In step 4, we inspect the sh.status() output and confirm that the chunk has been split. In step 5, we wish to move a chunk from shard0001 to shard0000. In order to do that, we run the sh.moveChunk() command with the collection name, the value of the key in the chunk which we wish to migrate, and the target shard ID. Finally, we start the balancer process and view the sh.status() output. We can observe that the chunk has been migrated to shard0000, as expected.

There are a lot of nuances when working with chunk migrations and it is highly recommended that you go through data partitioning guidelines mentioned at: https://docs.mongodb.com/manual/core/sharding-data-partitioning/.

Moving non-sharded collection data from one shard to another

In this recipe, we will look at how to migrate non-sharded data to another shard.

Getting ready

We need a sharded cluster, preferably the one we created in the previous recipe.

How to do it...

1. Connect to the mongos service and inspect the shard status:

   ```
   use myShardedDB

   sh.status()

   --- Sharding Status ---
    <-- output truncated -->
    databases:
    { "_id" : "myShardedDB", "primary" : "shard0002", "partitioned" : true }
    <-- output truncated -->
   ```

2. Insert a document in the new (non-sharded) collection of the sharded database:

   ```
   db.my_col.insert({foo: 'bar'})
   ```

3. Confirm that the document was stored on the primary shard by fetching the document:

   ```
   db.my_col.find({foo: 'bar'}).explain()['queryPlanner']['winningPlan']

   {
    "stage" : "SINGLE_SHARD",
   ```

```
"shards" : [
{
"shardName" : "shard0002",
"<--output truncated-->
```

4. Switch the primary to a different shard:

   ```
   use admin

   mongos> db.runCommand( { movePrimary: 'myShardedDB', to: 'shard0000' } )

   { "primary" : "shard0000:192.168.200.200:27027", "ok" : 1 }
   ```

5. Check that the migration has completed and the (non-sharded) collection is now on the new primary:

   ```
   sh.status()

   --- Sharding Status ---

   <-- output truncated -->

   databases:

   { "_id" : "myShardedDB", "primary" : "shard0000", "partitioned" : true }

   <-- output truncated -->

   use myShardedDB

   db.my_col.find({foo: 'bar'}).explain()['queryPlanner']['winningPlan']
   {
   "stage" : "SINGLE_SHARD",
   "shards" : [
   {
   "shardName" : "shard0000",
   <-- output truncated -->
   ```

How it works...

In a sharded cluster, MongoDB selects one node as the primary shard. Any data that is not part of the sharded collection is stored on the primary shard. In step 1, we connect to the mongos service running on the sharded cluster and inspect the shard status by running the `sh.status()` command. In the given sample output of this command, we can observe that the current primary shard is `shard0002`. Next, in step 2, we insert a document in the `my_col` collection of `myShardedDB`.

As this collection does not exist, a new collection is created on the primary shard (`shard0002`) and the document is inserted into it. This can be confirmed in step 3, when we run the `find()` command, followed by the `explain()` command.

In step 4, we select the admin database and issue the `movePrimary` command. In that, we provide the database name and the target shard which should become the new primary. Once this command is executed, MongoDB makes `shard0000` (in our example) the primary shard and begins copying the data to this new node. In step 5, we can confirm this by running the `sh.status()` command, as well as running the `find()` command.

In a production environment, there is a high chance that you will have multiple collections. It is imperative to plan the primary shard such that it can hold the additional (non-sharded) collections along with the chunks of the sharded collections. It is advisable to have the primary shard (or its replica set) run on servers that have additional resources to regular shards, such that the query overhead of non-sharded collections can be accommodated without any negative performance impact.

Removing a shard from the cluster

In this recipe, we will look at how to remove a shard from an existing cluster.

Getting ready

We need a sharded cluster, preferably the one we created in the *Managing chunks* recipe of this chapter.

How to do it...

1. Connect to the cluster's mongos service and view the current shards and their respective chunks:

   ```
   sh.status()

   --- Sharding Status ---

    sharding version: {
         "_id" : 1,
         "minCompatibleVersion" : 5,
         "currentVersion" : 6,
         "clusterId" : ObjectId("59c7950c9be3cff24816915a")
   }

    shards:
         {  "_id" : "shard0000",  "host" : "192.168.200.200:27027", "state" : 1 }
         {  "_id" : "shard0001",  "host" : "192.168.200.200:27028", "state" : 1 }
         {  "_id" : "shard0002",  "host" : "192.168.200.200:27029", "state" : 1 }

   <-- output truncated -->

    databases:
                                       shard0000    2
                                       shard0001    1
                                       shard0002    2
                         { "age" : { "$minKey" : 1 } } -->> { "age" : 18 } on : shard0000 Timestamp(2, 0)
                         { "age" : 18 } -->> { "age" : 50 } on : shard0001 Timestamp(4, 1)
                         { "age" : 50 } -->> { "age" : 54 } on : shard0000 Timestamp(4, 0)
                         { "age" : 54 } -->> { "age" : 73 } on : shard0002 Timestamp(3, 1)
                         { "age" : 73 } -->> { "age" : { "$maxKey" : 1 } } on : shard0002 Timestamp(1, 4)
   ```

2. Switch to the `admin` database and run the `removeShard` command:

   ```
   db.adminCommand({removeShard: 'shard0002'})

   {
   "msg" : "draining started successfully",
   "state" : "started",
   "shard" : "shard0002",
   "note" : "you need to drop or movePrimary these databases",
   "dbsToMove" : [ ],
   "ok" : 1
   }
   ```

3. Check the status of removal:

   ```
   db.adminCommand({removeShard: 'shard0002'})

   {
   "msg" : "draining ongoing",
   "state" : "ongoing",
   "remaining" : {
   "chunks" : NumberLong(1),
   "dbs" : NumberLong(0)
   },
   "note" : "you need to drop or movePrimary these databases",
   "dbsToMove" : [ ],
   "ok" : 1
   }

   db.adminCommand({removeShard: 'shard0002'})

   {
   "msg" : "removeshard completed successfully",
   "state" : "completed",
   "shard" : "shard0002",
   "ok" : 1
   }
   ```

4. Confirm that the shard was removed and chunks migrated:

```
sh.status()

--- Sharding Status ---
 sharding version: {
 "_id" : 1,
 "minCompatibleVersion" : 5,
 "currentVersion" : 6,
 "clusterId" : ObjectId("59c7950c9be3cff24816915a")
 }
 shards:
 { "_id" : "shard0000", "host" : "192.168.200.200:27027", "state" : 1 }
 { "_id" : "shard0001", "host" : "192.168.200.200:27028", "state" : 1 }
 <-- output truncated -->
 chunks:
 shard0000 3
 shard0001 2
 { "age" : { "$minKey" : 1 } } -->> { "age" : 18 } on : shard0000 Timestamp(2, 0)
 { "age" : 18 } -->> { "age" : 50 } on : shard0001 Timestamp(4, 1)
 { "age" : 50 } -->> { "age" : 54 } on : shard0000 Timestamp(4, 0)
 { "age" : 54 } -->> { "age" : 73 } on : shard0001 Timestamp(5, 0)
 { "age" : 73 } -->> { "age" : { "$maxKey" : 1 } } on : shard0000 Timestamp(6, 0)
```

How it works...

Removing a shard is a fairly straightforward operation. We begin by connecting to the cluster and inspecting the list of shards. In the sample output, we can observe that there are three shards in the cluster, each with one or more chunks assigned to it. In step 2, we switch to the 'admin' database and run the `removeShard` command, followed by the ID of the shard which we wish to remove. As soon as this command is entered, the balancer process immediately starts migrating the chunks to new shards. We can confirm this by the output of the command, in that, MongoDB gives a verbose message `draining started successfully`. This process would lock the collection and begin migrating the chunks to neighboring shards. In step 3, we run the same command again to view the status of the migration.

Depending on various factors, such as server resources and network bandwidth, the chunk migration can take time. In our case, you can observe that when we run the command for the second time, the status message says `draining ongoing`, and if we run it again (after a while), the message indicates that `removeshard completed successfully`. The latter message indicates that the chunks were migrated and the shard was successfully removed. In step 4, we can confirm this by observing the output of `sh.status()`, which indicates that the shard is no longer listed in the shards section and there are only two shards in the cluster. The two chunks on `shard0002` have been migrated to other shards.

> **TIP**
> In case you wish to remove the primary shard, you first need to migrate chunks and non-sharded data off the primary by running the `movePrimary` command. Once completed, you can execute the `removeShard` command to remove the shard.

Understanding tag aware sharding – zones

In this recipe, we will be looking at MongoDB's shard zones. A zone is essentially a group of shards based on a specific set of tags. Zones can help the distribution of chunks based on tags, across shards. All reads and writes, pertaining to documents within a zone, are performed on shards matching that zone. There can be various scenarios where zone based sharded clusters can prove to be highly useful. For example:

- An application that is geographically distributed would require that the frontend, as well as the data store, is close to the user

- The application has a multi-tier hardware architecture such that certain records are fetched from a higher tier (low latency) hardware whereas others could be fetched from a low tier (high latency inducing) hardware

> If a document does not match any configured zone, MongoDB will write it to any chunk in the cluster.

Getting ready

We need a sharded cluster, preferably the one we created in the *Managing chunk* recipe of this chapter.

How to do it...

1. Connect to the sharded cluster's mongos service and view the current shard status:

   ```
   sh.status()
   
   --- Sharding Status ---
   <-- output truncated -->
   
   chunks:
   
   shard0000   2
   shard0001   2
   shard0002   1
   
   { "age" : { "$minKey" : 1 } } -->> { "age" : 18 } on : shard0002 Timestamp(7, 0)
   { "age" : 18 } -->> { "age" : 50 } on : shard0001 Timestamp(4, 1)
   { "age" : 50 } -->> { "age" : 54 } on : shard0000 Timestamp(7, 1)
   { "age" : 54 } -->> { "age" : 73 } on : shard0001 Timestamp(5, 0)
   { "age" : 73 } -->> { "age" : { "$maxKey" : 1 } } on : shard0000 Timestamp(6, 0)
   ```

2. Create new tags:

   ```
   sh.addShardTag('shard0000', 'Zone-A')
   sh.addShardTag('shard0001', 'Zone-B')
   sh.addShardTag('shard0002', 'Zone-C')
   ```

3. Assign ranges to tags:

   ```
   sh.addTagRange('myShardedDB.users', {age: MinKey}, {age: 50}, 'Zone-A')
   sh.addTagRange('myShardedDB.users', {age: 50}, {age: 54}, 'Zone-B')
   sh.addTagRange('myShardedDB.users', {age: 54}, {age: MaxKey}, 'Zone-C')
   ```

4. View the shard status:

   ```
   sh.status()
   
   <-- output truncated -->
   
   chunks:
   
   shard0000   2
   ```

```
shard0001 1
shard0002 2

{ "age" : { "$minKey" : 1 } } -->> { "age" : 18 } on : shard0000
Timestamp(11, 1)
{ "age" : 18 } -->> { "age" : 50 } on : shard0000 Timestamp(8, 0)
{ "age" : 50 } -->> { "age" : 54 } on : shard0001 Timestamp(12, 1)
{ "age" : 54 } -->> { "age" : 73 } on : shard0002 Timestamp(12, 0)
{ "age" : 73 } -->> { "age" : { "$maxKey" : 1 } } on : shard0002

Timestamp(11, 0)

tag: Zone-A { "age" : { "$minKey" : 1 } } -->> { "age" : 50 }
tag: Zone-B { "age" : 50 } -->> { "age" : 54 }
tag: Zone-C { "age" : 54 } -->> { "age" : { "$maxKey" : 1 } }
```

How it works...

To begin, in step 1 we connect to the mongos instance of our sharded cluster and view the current distribution of chunks across the shards.

Next, in step 2, we create three tags: `Zone-A`, `Zone-B`, and `Zone-C`, and simultaneously add them to `shard0000`, `shard0001`, and `shard0002` respectively. At this point, only the tag is created and associated with each individual node. We now need to associate a shard key range with these tags. In step 3, we use the `sh.addTagRange()` command to associate the range to a tag.

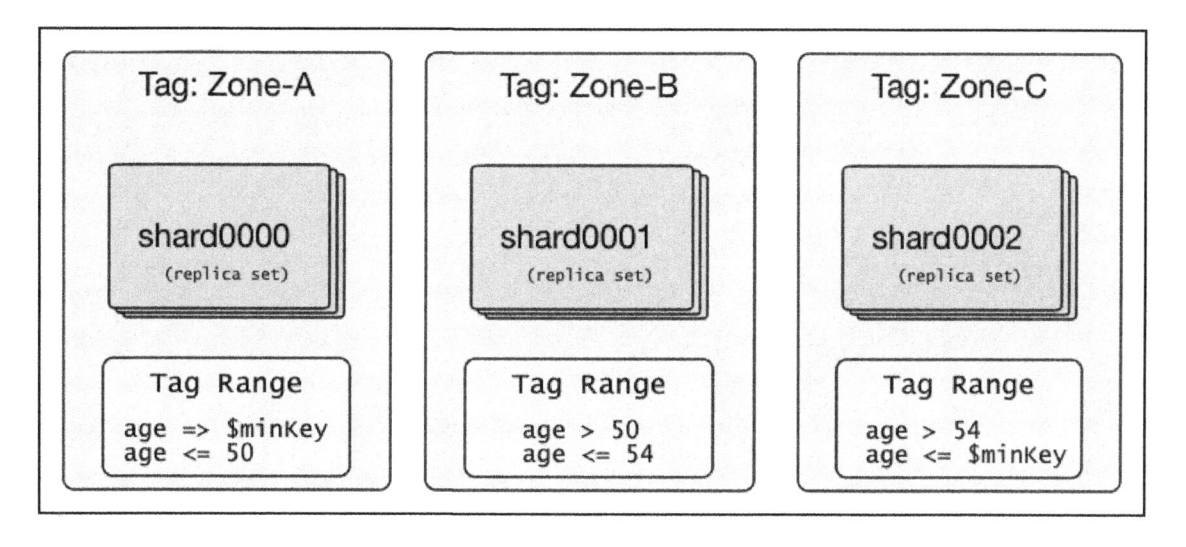

The command's first parameter is the collection name, followed by the minimum and maximum value of the shard key's range. Finally, it takes the name of the tag. The keywords `MinKey` and `MaxKey` are reserved MongoDB keywords, used to denote the lowest and the uppermost bounds of a range key.

Finally, in step 4, we rerun the `sh.status()` command, and by looking at the databases section of the output, we can confirm that the zones were indeed created with appropriate ranges assigned to them.

See also

For more examples, do have a look at MongoDBR17's official documentation at: `https://docs.mongodb.com/manual/core/zone-sharding/`.

This brings us to the end of the chapter. I will be extensively covering backup and monitoring of MongoDB shards in later chapters.

6
Managing MongoDB Backups

In this chapter, we will cover the following recipes:

- Taking backup using mongodump tool
- Taking backup of a specific MongoDB database or collection
- Taking backup of a small subset of documents in a collection
- Using bsondump tool to view mongodump output in human readable form
- Creating a point in time backup of replica sets
- Using the mongoexport tool
- Creating a backup of a sharded cluster

Introduction

Two core traits of a well designed database system are consistency of data and ability to restore data from a known good state. In MongoDB, the former part is mostly managed by the underlying server software. For example, using features like write concerns can also help ensure that writes received by the cluster are acknowledged under the predefined conditions. However, the ability to restore data is, for the most part, still a system that heavily relies on backup and restore strategies designed by database administrators. In this chapter, we will be looking at various tools and techniques that would hopefully help you in designing your optimal backup strategy.

Taking backup using mongodump tool

In this recipe, we will be looking at how to take MongoDB backups using `mongodump` utility. This utility is a part of the MongoDB binary package and is usually available in the `bin` directory of the binary package. If you have installed MongoDB using a package management tool, like Ubuntu's `apt` or Red Hats `yum`, then the utility can simply be invoked by typing `mongodump` in the console.

Getting ready

You need a single node MongoDB installation, preferably with some data in it. Refer to the recipe *Creating an index* in `Chapter 2`, *Understanding and Managing Indexes*, to learn how to import sample data into a MongoDB instance.

How to do it...

1. Create a directory to store the backups:

    ```
    mkdir /backups/
    ```

2. Switch to the directory and execute the `mongodump` utility:

    ```
    cd /backups/
    ```

3. Execute the command:

    ```
    mongodump
    ```

4. Your output should be similar to this:

    ```
    2017-10-04T03:26:34.251+0000 writing mydb.mockdata
    2017-10-04T03:26:34.459+0000 done dumping mydb.mockdata (100000 documents)
    ```

5. Examine the `dump` directory:

    ```
    ls -al dump/
    ```

6. You should see an output similar to this:

    ```
    drwxr-xr-x 2 root root 4096 Oct  4 03:29 mydb
    ```

7. Inspect the subdirectory:

   `ls -ahl dump/mydb/`

8. You should see an output similar to this:

   ```
   -rw-r--r-- 1 root root 13M Oct 4 03:27 mockdata.bson
   -rw-r--r-- 1 root root 85 Oct 4 03:27 mockdata.metadata.json
   ```

9. Remove the dump directory:

   `rm -rf /backups/dump`

10. Execute mongodump utility again with compression enabled:

    `mongodump --gzip --out /backups/dump`

11. You should see an output similar to this:

    ```
    2017-10-04T03:32:52.203+0000 writing mydb.mockdata
    2017-10-04T03:32:53.036+0000 done dumping mydb.mockdata (100000 documents)
    ```

12. Examine the directory:

    `ls -alh /backups/dump/mydb/`

13. You should see an output similar to this:

    ```
    -rw-r--r-- 1 root root 2.8M Oct 4 03:44 mockdata.bson.gz
    -rw-r--r-- 1 root root 100 Oct 4 03:44 mockdata.metadata.json.gz
    ```

14. Execute mongodump utility to create an archive with compression enabled:

    `mongodump --gzip --archive=/backups/mydb.archive`

15. You should see an output similar to this:

    ```
    2017-10-04T03:45:54.976+0000 writing mydb.mockdata to archive '/backups/mydb.archive'
    2017-10-04T03:45:55.705+0000 done dumping mydb.mockdata (100000 documents)
    ```

16. Examine the archive:

    `ls -alh /backups`

17. You should see an output similar to this:

    ```
    -rw-r--r-- 1 root root 2.8M Oct 4 03:45 mydb.archive
    ```

How it works...

The `mongodump` utility primarily connects to the mongod or mongos instance and dumps all data (except the local database) in BSON format.

In step 1, we create a common directory to store our backups and in step 2, we switch to that directory and execute the `mongodump` utility without any parameters.

By default, if no parameters are specified to the utility, `mongodump` creates a directory called `dump` in the current working directory. Additionally, for every database on the server, it creates a subdirectory with the name of the database and, within this subdirectory, it creates a BSON file for every collection within the database. We can observe this by inspecting the directories, as shown in step 3.

In addition to BSON files, mongodump also creates metadata files corresponding to the collection. If you inspect the file `/backups/dump/mydb/mockdata.metadata.json`, you should see the additional metadata (in this case, the index details) of this collection:

```
{"options":{},"indexes":[{"v":1,"key":{"_id":1},"name":"_id_","ns":"mydb.mockdata"}]}
```

Next, in step 4, we empty the directory and in step 5, we execute the `mongodump` utility with two command line parameters. The `--gzip` option enables compression and `--out` allows us to explicitly mention the path where the `dump` directory should be created.

In step 6, by examining the directory `/backups/dump/mydb/`, we can observe that the files are now compressed and have a `.gz` extension. If you compare the file size from the previous output, you can observe a substantial reduction in size. It goes without saying that compression of backups can greatly reduce the disk utilization of backups, as well as reducing transfer times when copying backups to remote location. However, if the dataset is too large, compression will incur a CPU overhead in addition to disk I/O. It is highly recommended to keep this in mind when you are planning your backup strategy. You may want to have a dedicated disk to store your backups.

Lastly, in step 7, we use the `--archive` flag, followed by the absolute filename of the archive. Starting with MongoDB Version 3.2, the `mongodump` utility supports creation of single file archives instead of directory based backups (as seen earlier).

As per the official documentation, archives have a slight benefit over directories, in that the restoration process is faster due to the contiguous nature of data in the file. Additionally, by adding the `--gzip` flag with `--archive`, we can ensure that the resulting archive file is compressed. This can be observed by examining the `/backups/` directory in step 8.

There's more...

The `mongodump` utility also supports printing the data in standard out (`STDOUT`) device. This allows additional possibilities, like using an alternate compression utility or transferring data to a remote server.

For example, the following command would create an archive and pipe it to `xz` compression utility. The latter would then create a `xz` compressed file.

```
mongodump --archive=- | xz --stdout > mydb.archive.xz
```

Another use case would be to transfer the archive over the wire to a remote location. An overly simple example is one in which you wish to take a backup on `Server-A` and copy it over to `Server-B`. You can run the following command on `Server-A`:

```
mongodump --gzip --archive=- | xz --stdout | ssh user@Server-B 'cat > /backups/mydb.archive.xz'
```

Taking backup of a specific mongodb database or collection

In this recipe, we will be using mongodump utility to take backups for a specific database and/or collection.

Getting ready

You need a single node MongoDB installation, preferably with some data in it. Refer to the recipe *Creating an index* in Chapter 2, *Understanding and Managing Indexes*, for instructions on how to import sample data into a MongoDB instance.

How to do it...

1. Open a mongo shell and examine the database:

    ```
    use mydb

    show collections
    ```

2. You should see the following output:

    ```
    mockdata
    system.indexes
    system.profile
    ```

3. Insert data into a random collection:

    ```
    db.tmpcol.insert({foo:1})
    ```

4. Use mongodump to take backup of specific database:

    ```
    mongodump --gzip -d mydb
    ```

5. You should see an output similar to this:

    ```
    2017-10-04T12:05:24.352+0000 writing mydb.mockdata
    2017-10-04T12:05:24.353+0000 writing mydb.tmpcol
    2017-10-04T12:05:24.361+0000 done dumping mydb.tmpcol (1 document)
    2017-10-04T12:05:25.098+0000 done dumping mydb.mockdata (100000 documents)
    ```

6. Use mongodump to take backup of specific collection:

    ```
    mongodump --gzip -d mydb -c mockdata
    ```

7. You should see an output similar to this:

    ```
    2017-10-04T11:56:37.357+0000 writing mydb.mockdata
    2017-10-04T11:56:38.082+0000 done dumping mydb.mockdata (100000 documents)
    ```

8. Take backup of the entire database, excluding a collection:

    ```
    mongodump --gzip -d mydb --excludeCollection=mockdata
    ```

9. You should see an output similar to this:

   ```
   2017-10-04T12:06:03.787+0000 writing mydb.tmpcol
   2017-10-04T12:06:03.788+0000 done dumping mydb.tmpcol (1 document)
   ```

How it works...

This recipe should be pretty straightforward to understand. Assuming you have loaded the sample data as mentioned in the *Getting ready* section, you should have a database called mydb with one collection called mockdata. In step 1, we create another collection in mydb, called tmpcol and insert a document in it.

Next, in step 2, we execute the mongodump utility with the -d parameter, followed by the name of the database we wish to backup. In step 3, we take a more specific backup by adding an additional flag -c, followed by the name of the collection which we wish to backup.

Finally, in step 4, we use --excludeCollection to backup the entire database, except for the collection mentioned with this parameter. This can be a handy switch when we want to exclude a particular collection when taking a backup.

Additionally, mongodump also comes with another flag, --excludeCollectionsWithPrefix. This flag can be used to exclude all collections which start with the string specified in its value.

Taking backup of a small subset of documents in a collection

In the previous recipe, we saw how to backup certain databases and their collections. In this recipe, we will look at how to use the mongodump utility to backup specific documents within a collection.

Getting ready

You need a single node MongoDB installation, preferably with some data in it. Refer to the recipe *Creating an index* in Chapter 2, *Understanding and Managing Indexes*, on how to import sample data into a MongoDB instance.

How to do it...

1. Open the mongo shell and check all documents for a specific language:

    ```
    use mydb
    ```

    ```
    db.mockdata.count({language:"Thai"})
    ```

2. You should see the following output:

    ```
    892
    ```

3. Add the following to `query.json`:

    ```
    {language: 'Thai'}
    ```

4. Execute the `mongodump` utility with a specific query:

    ```
    mongodump -d mydb -c mockdata --queryFile query.json
    ```

5. You should see the following output:

    ```
    2017-10-04T12:17:28.559+0000 writing mydb.mockdata
    2017-10-04T12:17:28.596+0000 done dumping mydb.mockdata (892 documents)
    ```

How it works...

By now, these steps should be quite verbose in explaining what they do. We begin by examining how many records are present in our `mockdata` collection for `{language:"Thai"}`. Next, we create a new JSON file called `query.json` and add the query line in it. In step 3, we execute the `mongodump` utility and specify the `--queryFile` parameter with the name of the file containing the query. As a query always has to run against a collection, we have to specify the database and the collection name as the values for the `-d` and `-c` flags, respectively.

Instead of using a query file, you can also provide the query inline by using the `--query` parameter. Here, the command, used in step 3, would look like:

```
mongodump -d mydb -c mockdata --query "{language: 'Thai'}"
```

Using bsondump tool to view mongodump output in human readable form

In this recipe, we will be using `bsondump` tool to examine the BSON files created by `mongodump` utility.

Getting ready

You need a single node MongoDB installation, preferably with some data in it. Refer to the recipe *Creating an index* in Chapter 2, *Understanding and Managing Indexes*, for instructions on how to import sample data into a MongoDB instance.

How to do it...

1. Take a backup of the `mockdata` collection:

   ```
   mongodump --gzip -d mydb -c mockdata --out /backups/dump
   ```

2. This should give the following output:

   ```
   2017-10-04T12:50:37.000+0000 writing mydb.mockdata
   2017-10-04T12:50:37.737+0000 done dumping mydb.mockdata (100000 documents)
   ```

3. Examine the backup directory:

   ```
   ls -al dump/mydb/
   ```

4. This should give the following output:

   ```
   -rw-r--r-- 1 root root 2836312 Oct 4 12:50 mockdata.bson.gz
   -rw-r--r-- 1 root root     100 Oct 4 12:50 mockdata.metadata.json.gz
   ```

5. Execute the `bsondump` utility to view the contents of the BSON file:

   ```
   zcat /backups/dump/mydb/mockdata.bson.gz | bsondump --pretty
   ```

Managing MongoDB Backups

6. This should give the following output:

```
<-- output truncated -->
{
        "_id": {
                "$oid": "59913879d574be2148cf8294"
        },
        "first_name": "Helenka",
        "last_name": "Gorries",
        "gender": "Female",
        "city": "Colcabamba",
        "language": "Quechua"
}
{
        "_id": {
                "$oid": "59913879d574be2148cf8296"
        },
        "first_name": "Derward",
        "last_name": "Sabbatier",
        "gender": "Male",
        "city": "Tindog",
        "language": "Maltese"
}
    <-- output truncated -->
```

How it works...

The `bsondump` utility is a handy tool bundled with all MongoDB packages. It is very useful to parse the binary BSON files and output them in human readable format. In step 1, we begin by taking a backup of the `mockdata` collection. As expected, in step 2, we can see that the collection's data was dumped into two files, namely, `mockdata.bson.gz` and `mockdata.metadata.json.gz`. The former contains the actual data in BSON format while the latter contains metadata (index information) of the collection.

At this stage, I would like to point out two limitations of the `bsondump` tool. First, it cannot read a compressed file, not even `.gzip`. Second, it cannot read a `mongodump` archive either. It can literally only read raw BSON files. So, in step 3, in order to conform to its requirements, we will use Linux's `zcat` utility, which prints a `.gzip` file, and pipe its output to `bsondump`. The additional `--pretty` flag is used to prettify the JSON output, so that it is easier to read. If you plan to run it through any scripts, you can omit this flag.

Creating a point in time backup of replica sets

MongoDB replica sets maintain operations log using a capped collection called oplog. The oplog is what is shared between the replica set nodes to maintain consistency. In this recipe, we will look at how to create point in time backups of replica sets using oplog.

Getting ready

You need a three node MongoDB replica set installation, preferably with some data in it. Refer to the recipes *Initializing a new replica set*, in `Chapter 4`, *High Availability with Replication*, for instructions on how to create a replica set, and *Creating an index* in `Chapter 2`, *Understanding and Managing Indexes*, for instructions on how to import sample data into a MongoDB instance.

How to do it...

1. First, we connect to the primary replica set node and insert about 100,000 random documents:

    ```
    for(var x=0; x<100000; x++){
    db.mycol.insert({age:(Math.round(Math.random()*100)%20) }) }
    ```

2. Immediately switch to a different Terminal and take the backup:

    ```
    mongodump --oplog --out /backups/dump/
    ```

3. You should see an output similar to this:

    ```
    2017-10-04T15:02:53.921+0000    writing admin.system.version
    2017-10-04T15:02:53.928+0000    done dumping admin.system.version (1 document)
    2017-10-04T15:02:53.929+0000    writing mydb.mockdata
    2017-10-04T15:02:53.934+0000    writing mydb.mycol
    2017-10-04T15:02:53.986+0000    done dumping mydb.mycol (5922 documents)
    2017-10-04T15:02:54.662+0000    done dumping mydb.mockdata (100000 documents)
    2017-10-04T15:02:54.667+0000    writing captured oplog
    2017-10-04T15:02:55.025+0000    dumped 941 oplog entries
    ```

4. Inspect the backup directory:

    ```
    ls -al /backups/dump/
    ```

5. You should see an output similar to this:

    ```
    drwxr-xr-x 2 root root   4096 Oct 4 14:37 admin
    drwxr-xr-x 2 root root   4096 Oct 4 14:37 mydb
    -rw-r--r-- 1 root root 106333 Oct 4 15:02 oplog.bson
    ```

6. Inspect the `oplog.bson` file:

    ```
    bsondump /backups/dump/oplog.bson
    ```

7. You should see an output similar to this:

    ```
    <-- output truncated -->
    {"ts":{"$timestamp":{"t":1507129375,"i":5}},"t":{"$numberLong":"104
    "},"h":{"$numberLong":"-6696408951828346681"},"v":2,"op":"i","ns":"
    mydb.mycol","o":{"_id":{"$oid":"59d4f81f1cfc955658fc1275"},"age":15
    .0}}
    {"ts":{"$timestamp":{"t":1507129375,"i":6}},"t":{"$numberLong":"104
    "},"h":{"$numberLong":"-2383386998191081659"},"v":2,"op":"i","ns":"
    mydb.mycol","o":{"_id":{"$oid":"59d4f81f1cfc955658fc1276"},"age":9.
    0}}
    2017-10-04T15:05:10.721+0000 941 objects found
    ```

How it works...

The point of this recipe is to demonstrate a scenario where a database backup is being taken while there are operations still being performed on the server. In order to simulate this, we begin by opening two terminal windows. In step 1, we open a mongo shell (in the first Terminal window) and run a simple JavaScript code snippet, which would insert about 100,000 documents. As soon as you initiate this code, immediately switch to the other Terminal window and execute the `mongodump` utility as shown in step 2. We explicitly mention the `--oplog` flag to ensure we capture the point in time oplog entries of operations that are being performed during the backup operation. This will create a file called `oplog.bson` in the top level directory, as shown in the output in step 3.

Finally, if you feel industrious, you can explore the `oplog.bson` file using the `bsondump` utility, as shown in step 4.

> **TIP**: When attempting to restore a backup using `mongorestore` utility, which contains oplogs, ensure you use the `--oplogReplay` flag.

Using the mongoexport tool

In this recipe, we will be looking at `mongoexport`, a utility provided to export MongoDB data in JSON and CSV format.

Getting ready

You need a single node MongoDB installation, preferably with some data in it. Refer to the recipe *Creating an index* in `Chapter 2`, *Understanding and Managing Indexes*, for instructions on how to import sample data into a MongoDB instance.

How to do it...

1. Execute the `mongoexport` utility with the following options:

   ```
   mongoexport -d mydb -c mockdata --fields
   first_name,last_name,language --query '{language: "English"}' --
   type csv > my_data.csv
   ```

2. Your output should be similar to this:

   ```
   2017-10-04T16:15:51.939+0000 connected to: localhost
   2017-10-04T16:15:51.981+0000 exported 866 records
   ```

3. Examine the contents file `my_data.csv`:

   ```
   first_name,last_name,language
   Gareth,Mott,English
   Pace,Goodram,English
   Valaree,Dickinson,English
   Nickola,Messer,English
   Ellene,Wardlaw,English
   Caryn,Petruk,English
   Alta,Major,English
   Sonya,Ritchman,English
   Howie,MacHostie,English
   ```

How it works...

The `mongoexport` utility is not really the ideal tool to use for performing backups on production databases. However, it can be used as a very nifty tool to quickly extract data for generating reports or (if you are confident) maybe a quick backup in JSON or CSV format.

In step 1, we execute the `mongoexport` utility with some options similar to `mongodump` utility. The flags are `-d` for the name of the database, `-c` for the name of the collection, `--fields` for the name of the fields which should be returned, `--query` for the query to perform on the collection, and lastly, `--type` for the output type. We pipe the output to a file called `my_data.csv` and, upon its inspection, we can observe that the tool has created a comma-separated CSV file with its first line containing the name of the fields representing the output.

Creating a backup of a sharded cluster

In this recipe, we will be looking at how to take a backup of a sharded MongoDB cluster. We will be looking at how to backup the config server and the relevant shards which contain the actual data.

Getting ready

You will need a sharded MongoDB cluster, with a minimum of a **config server replica set** (**CSRS**) and one shard. Refer to the recipe *Setting up and configuring a sharded cluster* in `Chapter 5`, *High Scalability with Sharding*, on how to create a sharded cluster.

How to do it...

1. Connect to the mongos server and stop the balancer:

   use config

   sh.stopBalancer()

2. Take a backup of the config server:

   mongodump -h localhost -p 27019 -d config --out /backups/configbkp

3. Take backup from the shard:

   mongodump -h localhost -p 27027 -d myShardedDB --out /backups/shard1bkp

4. Connect back to the mongos server and enable the balancer:

   use config

   sh.startBalancer()

How it works...

Taking backups of a sharded cluster is a bit nuanced, as it involves ensuring certain steps are considered before planning a backup strategy. For starters, we need to stop the balancer. We begin by connecting to mongos server and stopping the balancer, as shown in step 1. Next, in step 2, we use mongodump to take a backup of the config server. In a production environment, prior to executing a mongodump, it is suggested to connect to the config server replica set secondary, issue a db.fsyncLock() and rs.slaveOk(). This ensures that there are no writes to the config database, of the given replica set and we are able to read from it. Next, in step 3, we connect to each shard (our example only has one shard member) and execute the mongodump utility to take the database backup from that shard. Lastly, we connect back to the mongos instance and start the balancer by running the sh.startBalancer() command.

7
Restoring MongoDB from Backups

In this chapter, we will cover the following recipes:

- Restoring standalone MongoDB databases using the mongorestore tool
- Restoring specific database or specific collection
- Restoring data from one collection or database to another
- Creating a new MongoDB replica set node using backups
- Restoring a MongoDB sharded cluster from backup

Introduction

In the previous chapter, we saw various tools and techniques used to back up MongoDB data. Continuing from that trail, this chapter should help you understand how to restore data from a given backup. For most restoration use cases, we will use the `mongorestore` utility that comes bundled with the MongoDB installation. Additionally, we will cover different types of MongoDB setups, ranging from standalone servers and replica sets to sharded databases. So, let's get started!

Restoring standalone MongoDB using the mongorestore tool

In this recipe, we will be looking at how to use the `mongorestore` tool to restore a previously generated backup.

Getting ready

You need a single-node MongoDB installation, preferably with some data in it. Refer to the *Creating an index* recipe in `Chapter 2`, *Understanding and Managing Indexes,* on how to import sample data into a MongoDB instance.

How to do it...

1. Connect to the MongoDB server via mongo shell, and insert about 1,000 random documents:

   ```
   for(var x=0; x<1000; x++){
   db.mycol.insert({age:(Math.round(Math.random()*100)%20) }) }
   ```

2. Immediately switch to a different Terminal, and take the backup:

   ```
   mongodump --out /backups/dump/
   ```

3. You should see output similar to this:

   ```
   2017-10-06T08:02:38.082+0000 writing admin.system.version
   2017-10-06T08:02:38.083+0000 done dumping admin.system.version (1 document)
   2017-10-06T08:02:38.083+0000 writing mydb.mockdata to
   2017-10-06T08:02:38.084+0000 writing mydb.mycol to
   2017-10-06T08:02:38.095+0000 done dumping mydb.mycol (1000 documents)
   2017-10-06T08:02:38.279+0000 done dumping mydb.mockdata (100000 documents
   ```

4. Switch back to the operating system's Terminal window, and execute the `mongorestore` utility:

   ```
   mongorestore --drop --dir /backups/dump/
   ```

5. You should see output similar to this:

   ```
   2017-10-06T08:29:10.775+0000 preparing collections to restore from
   2017-10-06T08:29:10.782+0000 reading metadata for mydb.mockdata from /backups/dump/mydb/mockdata.metadata.json
   2017-10-06T08:29:10.786+0000 reading metadata for mydb.mycol from /backups/dump/mydb/mycol.metadata.json
   2017-10-06T08:29:10.795+0000 restoring mydb.mycol from /backups/dump/mydb/mycol.bson
   ```

```
2017-10-06T08:29:10.809+0000 restoring mydb.mockdata from
/backups/dump/mydb/mockdata.bson
2017-10-06T08:29:10.861+0000 no indexes to restore
2017-10-06T08:29:10.861+0000 finished restoring mydb.mycol (1000
documents)
2017-10-06T08:29:13.772+0000 [################.......]
mydb.mockdata  8.62MB/12.2MB  (71.0%)
2017-10-06T08:29:15.211+0000 [########################]
mydb.mockdata  12.2MB/12.2MB  (100.0%)
2017-10-06T08:29:15.211+0000 no indexes to restore
2017-10-06T08:29:15.211+0000 finished restoring mydb.mockdata
(100000 documents)
2017-10-06T08:29:15.211+0000 done
```

How it works...

We begin simply by adding another collection to the existing mydb database, just to increase the sample dataset for verbosity. In step 2, we take a database backup by executing the mongodump utility with no special parameters other than the output directory. Next, in step 3, we execute the mongorestore utility with two parameters. The --drop parameter is used to drop the collection before importing. We are using it primarily to avoid duplicate key errors, which would occur because the backup contains the _id fields. As the _id field is unique, the database restoration process would yield duplicate key errors. In a real-world scenario, you should be extremely careful when adding a --drop collection flag. The mongorestore utility is also provided with the --dir flag, which points to the directory containing the backup files. The utility will go through each subdirectory within the supplied directory, read the files present in that directory, and restore the respective collections. Any indexes taken during the backup are also restored. If you had provided a --gzip option when executing mongodump, you can provide the same flag with the mongorestore utility, allowing it to recognize the backup as a set of GZIP compressed files. Likewise, if you are restoring from an archive, you can use the --archive file instead of the --dir parameter.

Last but not least, if you are ever in doubt, you can always use the --dryRun option which provides extra verbose output like this:

```
mongorestore --dryRun -vvv --dir /backups/dump
```

The preceding command executes the entire process of database restoration without actually restoring the data. This can prove extremely useful when you wish to double-check the integrity of your data and the restoration parameters.

Restoring specific database or specific collection

In this recipe, we will explore the options of `mongorestore` utility that allow us to restore backups for a specific database or collection. We will also look at how to exclude certain collections or databases during restoration.

Getting ready

You need a single-node MongoDB installation, preferably with some data in it. Refer to the *Creating an index* recipe in `Chapter 2`, *Understanding and Managing Indexes*, on how to import sample data into a MongoDB instance.

How to do it...

1. Connect to the MongoDB server via mongo shell, and insert about 1,000 random documents:

   ```
   for(var x=0; x<1000; x++){
   db.mycol.insert({age:(Math.round(Math.random()*100)%20) }) }
   ```

2. Immediately switch to a different Terminal, and take the backup:

   ```
   mongodump --out /backups/dump/
   ```

3. You should see output similar to this:

   ```
   2017-10-06T08:02:38.082+0000 writing admin.system.version
   2017-10-06T08:02:38.083+0000 done dumping admin.system.version (1 document)
   2017-10-06T08:02:38.083+0000 writing mydb.mockdata to
   2017-10-06T08:02:38.084+0000 writing mydb.mycol to
   2017-10-06T08:02:38.095+0000 done dumping mydb.mycol (1000 documents)
   2017-10-06T08:02:38.279+0000 done dumping mydb.mockdata (100000 documents
   ```

Restoring MongoDB from Backups

4. Switch back to the operating system's Terminal window, and execute the `mongorestore` utility to only restore a single collection:

   ```
   mongorestore --drop -v --dir /backups/dump --nsInclude
   'mydb.mockdata'
   ```

5. You should see output similar to this:

   ```
   2017-10-08T10:45:43.108+0000 using --dir flag instead of arguments
   2017-10-08T10:45:43.113+0000 using write concern: w='majority',
   j=false, fsync=false, wtimeout=0
   2017-10-08T10:45:43.114+0000 preparing collections to restore from
   2017-10-08T10:45:43.115+0000 found collection mydb.mockdata bson to
   restore to mydb.mockdata
   2017-10-08T10:45:43.116+0000 found collection metadata from
   mydb.mockdata to restore to mydb.mockdata
   2017-10-08T10:45:43.117+0000 dropping collection mydb.mockdata
   before restoring
   2017-10-08T10:45:43.121+0000 reading metadata for mydb.mockdata
   from /backups/dump/mydb/mockdata.metadata.json
   2017-10-08T10:45:43.126+0000 creating collection mydb.mockdata
   using options from metadata
   2017-10-08T10:45:43.134+0000 restoring mydb.mockdata from
   /backups/dump/mydb/mockdata.bson
   2017-10-08T10:45:46.110+0000 [#################.......]
   mydb.mockdata 9.23MB/12.2MB (76.0%)
   2017-10-08T10:45:47.083+0000 [########################]
   mydb.mockdata 12.2MB/12.2MB (100.0%)
   2017-10-08T10:45:47.083+0000 no indexes to restore
   2017-10-08T10:45:47.083+0000 finished restoring mydb.mockdata
   (100000 documents)
   2017-10-08T10:45:47.083+0000 done
   ```

6. Execute `mongorestore` to exclude a collection during restoration:

   ```
   mongorestore -v --drop --dir /backups/dump --nsExclude
   'mydb.mockdata'
   ```

7. You should see output similar to this:

   ```
   2017-10-08T10:47:00.053+0000 using --dir flag instead of arguments
   2017-10-08T10:47:00.059+0000 using write concern: w='majority',
   j=false, fsync=false, wtimeout=0
   2017-10-08T10:47:00.060+0000 preparing collections to restore from
   2017-10-08T10:47:00.061+0000 found collection admin.system.version
   bson to restore to admin.system.version
   2017-10-08T10:47:00.062+0000 found collection metadata from
   ```

Restoring MongoDB from Backups

```
admin.system.version to restore to admin.system.version
2017-10-08T10:47:00.063+0000 found collection mydb.mycol bson to
restore to mydb.mycol
2017-10-08T10:47:00.064+0000 found collection metadata from
mydb.mycol to restore to mydb.mycol
2017-10-08T10:47:00.065+0000 dropping collection mydb.mycol before
restoring
2017-10-08T10:47:00.069+0000 reading metadata for mydb.mycol from
/backups/dump/mydb/mycol.metadata.json
2017-10-08T10:47:00.076+0000 creating collection mydb.mycol using
options from metadata
2017-10-08T10:47:00.082+0000 restoring mydb.mycol from
/backups/dump/mydb/mycol.bson
2017-10-08T10:47:00.120+0000 no indexes to restore
2017-10-08T10:47:00.120+0000 finished restoring mydb.mycol (1000
documents)
2017-10-08T10:47:00.120+0000 done
```

How it works...

We begin simply by adding another collection to the existing `mydb` database, just to increase the sample dataset for verbosity. In step 2, we take a database backup by executing the `mongodump` utility with no special parameters other than the output directory.

Now comes the interesting bit. If you recall from Chapter 6, *Managing MongoDB Backups*, you saw the use of the `mongodump` utility with the `-d` and `-c` flags, which correspond to database and collection, respectively. As of MongoDB 3.4, the `mongorestore` utility uses the namespace flags instead. A namespace is a dot (.) separated tuple of two words, first being the database name and the other, the collection or index name. For example, `mydb.mockdata` would denote the namespace for the `mockdata` collection in the `mydb` database. This nomenclature allows a slightly more usable denotation of a parent-child type of relationship between a database and its subobjects. In step 3, we use the `--nsInclude` flag to explicitly specify the namespace that we wish to restore. In our case, it is `mydb.mockdata` as the namespace that denotes the database and collection names.

In step 4, we use the `--nsExclude` flag to explicitly exclude a given collection while restoring data.

> **TIP**
> Namespaces can contain wildcards as well, for example, you can use the `mydb.m*` namespace to restore all collections within the `mydb` database that start with the letter m.

Restoring data from one collection or database to another

In this recipe, we will look at how to use the `mongorestore` utility to restore data from one collection to another.

Getting ready

You need a single-node MongoDB installation, preferably with some data in it. Refer to the *Creating an index* recipe in `Chapter 2`, *Understanding and Managing Indexes*, on how to import sample data into a MongoDB instance.

How to do it...

1. Connect to the MongoDB server via mongo shell, and insert about 1,000 random documents:

    ```
    for(var x=0; x<1000; x++){
    db.mycol.insert({age:(Math.round(Math.random()*100)%20) }) }
    ```

2. Immediately switch to a different Terminal, and take the backup:

    ```
    mongodump --out /backups/dump/
    ```

3. You should see output similar to this:

    ```
    2017-10-06T08:02:38.082+0000 writing admin.system.version to
    2017-10-06T08:02:38.083+0000 done dumping admin.system.version (1 document)
    2017-10-06T08:02:38.083+0000 writing mydb.mockdata to
    2017-10-06T08:02:38.084+0000 writing mydb.mycol to
    2017-10-06T08:02:38.095+0000 done dumping mydb.mycol (1000 documents)
    2017-10-06T08:02:38.279+0000 done dumping mydb.mockdata (100000 documents)
    ```

4. Switch back to the operating system's Terminal window, and execute the `mongorestore` utility to restore data from one collection to another:

    ```
    mongorestore -v --dir /backups/dump --nsInclude 'mydb.mockdata' --nsFrom 'mydb.mockdata' --nsTo 'newdb.mockdata'
    ```

Restoring MongoDB from Backups

5. You should see output similar to this:

   ```
   2017-10-08T12:25:18.460+0000 using --dir flag instead of arguments
   2017-10-08T12:25:18.466+0000 using write concern: w='majority',
   j=false, fsync=false, wtimeout=0
   2017-10-08T12:25:18.467+0000 preparing collections to restore from
   2017-10-08T12:25:18.468+0000 found collection mydb.mockdata bson to
   restore to newdb.mockdata
   2017-10-08T12:25:18.468+0000 found collection metadata from
   mydb.mockdata to restore to newdb.mockdata
   2017-10-08T12:25:18.469+0000 reading metadata for newdb.mockdata
   from /backups/dump/mydb/mockdata.metadata.json
   2017-10-08T12:25:18.470+0000 creating collection newdb.mockdata
   using options from metadata
   2017-10-08T12:25:18.476+0000 restoring newdb.mockdata from
   /backups/dump/mydb/mockdata.bson
   2017-10-08T12:25:21.462+0000 [###############........]
   newdb.mockdata  8.38MB/12.2MB  (69.0%)
   2017-10-08T12:25:22.856+0000 [########################]
   newdb.mockdata  12.2MB/12.2MB  (100.0%)
   2017-10-08T12:25:22.857+0000 no indexes to restore
   2017-10-08T12:25:22.858+0000 finished restoring newdb.mockdata
   (100000 documents)
   2017-10-08T12:25:22.859+0000 done
   ```

6. Execute the `mongorestore` utility to restore data from multiple collections' backups to a new collection:

   ```
   mongorestore -v --dir /backups/dump --nsInclude 'mydb.mockdata' --nsFrom 'mydb.$colname$' --nsTo 'mydb.copyof_$colname$'
   ```

7. You should see output similar to this:

   ```
   2017-10-08T12:26:29.037+0000 using --dir flag instead of arguments
   2017-10-08T12:26:29.048+0000 using write concern: w='majority',
   j=false, fsync=false, wtimeout=0
   2017-10-08T12:26:29.049+0000 preparing collections to restore from
   2017-10-08T12:26:29.050+0000 found collection mydb.mockdata bson to
   restore to mydb.copyof_mockdata
   2017-10-08T12:26:29.051+0000 found collection metadata from
   mydb.mockdata to restore to mydb.copyof_mockdata
   2017-10-08T12:26:29.053+0000 reading metadata for
   mydb.copyof_mockdata from /backups/dump/mydb/mockdata.metadata.json
   2017-10-08T12:26:29.054+0000 creating collection
   mydb.copyof_mockdata using options from metadata
   2017-10-08T12:26:29.070+0000 restoring mydb.copyof_mockdata from
   /backups/dump/mydb/mockdata.bson
   ```

```
2017-10-08T12:26:32.045+0000 [################......]
mydb.copyof_mockdata  9.23MB/12.2MB  (76.0%)
2017-10-08T12:26:32.725+0000 [########################]
mydb.copyof_mockdata  12.2MB/12.2MB  (100.0%)
2017-10-08T12:26:32.725+0000 no indexes to restore
2017-10-08T12:26:32.725+0000 finished restoring
mydb.copyof_mockdata (100000 documents)
2017-10-08T12:26:32.725+0000 done
```

How it works...

We begin simply by adding another collection to the existing mydb database, just to increase the sample dataset for verbosity. In step 2, we take a database backup by executing the mongodump utility with no special parameters other than the output directory.

In step 3, we use two new parameters-- --nsFrom and --nsTo. The value of the --nsFrom parameter indicates the namespace from which the restoration is supposed to be renamed, and the value of --nsTo indicates the target namespace. In our example, we are restoring the backup of data from mydb.mockdata to a new database newdb.mockdata. You may have noticed that I am still using the --nsInclude flag with the mydb.mockdata value. This ensures that the mongorestore utility is only considering the mydb.mockdata namespace and no other databases or collections. In the absence of these parameters, the mongodrestore utility will restore all the backups in the --dir path. So to restrict its scope to only the relevant database and collection, we have to use the --nsInclude flag.

Finally, in step 4, we use the utility's feature of allowing variable substitution in renaming namespaces. Let's break down the flags and their values used in this step:

Flag	Value	Effect
--nsInclude	mydb.mockdata	Restrict match to database mydb and collection mockdata.
--nsFrom	mydb.$colname$	For each collection matched by --nsInclude, match for database mydb and store the collection name in a variable called $colname$.

| `--nsTo` | `mydb.copyof_$colname$` | For each collection returned by `--nsFrom`, restore data to the namespace `mydb.copyof_$colname$`, where the variable `$colname$` is replaced by its value. For example, `mydb.mockdata` would get restored as `mydb.copyof_mockdata`. |

This little trick can be very useful in the following scenarios:

- You need to test index behavior without affecting the actual data
- Set up a copy of your data on the same server in a development environment

Creating a new MongoDB replica set node using backups

In this recipe, we will look at how to set up a new replica set using a previously generated backup.

Getting ready

All you need is a MongoDB backup, preferably one generated in the *Taking backup using mongodump tool* recipe of Chapter 6, *Managing MongoDB Backups*. For this example, we will assume the database backup is present in `/backups/dump/`. Additionally, we will create individual directories for each mongod instance:

```
mkdir -p /data/server{1,2,3}/db
```

How to do it...

1. Start a single-node replica set:

    ```
    mongod --dbpath /data/server1/db --replSet MyReplicaSet --port 27017
    ```

2. Connect to the replica set and initiate the database:

   ```
   rs.initiate()
   ```

3. You should see output similar to this:

   ```
   {
           "info2" : "no configuration specified. Using a default configuration for the set",
           "me" : "192.168.200.200:27017",
           "ok" : 1
   }
   ```

4. Use the `mongorestore` utility to restore the database:

   ```
   mongorestore --dir /backups/dump/
   ```

5. You should see output similar to this:

   ```
   2017-10-08T13:25:17.215+0000 preparing collections to restore from
   2017-10-08T13:25:17.216+0000 reading metadata for mydb.mockdata from /backups/dump/mydb/mockdata.metadata.json
   2017-10-08T13:25:17.226+0000 restoring mydb.mockdata from /backups/dump/mydb/mockdata.bson
   2017-10-08T13:25:17.252+0000 no indexes to restore
   2017-10-08T13:25:18.385+0000 finished restoring mydb.mockdata (100000 documents)
   2017-10-08T13:25:18.385+0000 done
   ```

6. Connect to the primary node using mongo shell, and shut down the replica set node:

   ```
   use admin

   db.shutdownServer({force: true})
   ```

7. Copy the data of the primary node to the `--dbpath` of the secondary nodes:

   ```
   cp -Rpf /data/server1/db/* /data/server2/db/

   cp -Rpf /data/server1/db/* /data/server3/db/
   ```

8. Start all three replica set nodes:

    ```
    mongod --dbpath /data/server1/db --replSet MyReplicaSet --port 27017

    mongod --dbpath /data/server2/db --replSet MyReplicaSet --port 27018

    mongod --dbpath /data/server3/db --replSet MyReplicaSet --port 27019
    ```

9. Connect to the primary node using mongo shell and add the secondary nodes, one at a time:

    ```
    rs.add('192.168.200.200:27018')

    rs.add('192.168.200.200:27019')
    ```

10. Check that the nodes in the replica set are now in sync:

    ```
    rs.status()
    ```

How it works...

We begin by starting a single-node replica set running on port 27017. Next, in step 2, we connect to this replica set instance and initialize the replica set using the `rs.initiate()` command. For step 3, we switch to a different console window and restore the database backup using the `mongorestore` utility. In step 4, we switch back to the mongo shell, which is connected to our replica set node, and shut down the server using the `db.shutdownServer({force: true})` command. By default, a replica set with no nodes will not shut down, so we use the `force:true` parameter to force it into bending the knee. In step 5, we copy the data from the primary instance's `--dbpath` to the respective paths for the other two instances. Next, in step 6, we start all three replica set instances with their respective `--dbpath` and `--port` parameters. In step 7, we connect to the primary replica set instance and add the other two instances. Lastly, we can check that the other two nodes have been added and are in sync using the `rs.status()` command.

Clearly, this is an overly simplified example of how to create a replica set from an existing backup. An alternate method would be to restore the backup on a single node, start the secondary nodes with no data in them, and simply add them to the replica set using the `rs.add()` command. As this method initiates an on-the-fly sync of data between the nodes, you should add the nodes one by one.

In a production environment, if the dataset is too large, it is rather preferred to do an initial sync using the data files and then let the nodes catch up with the primary node, once they are added.

Restoring a MongoDB sharded cluster from backup

In this recipe, we will be looking at how to restore a sharded cluster from a previously generated backup.

Getting ready

You will need a sharded cluster, with a minimum of a **config server replica set** (**CSRS**) and one shard. Refer to the *Setting up and configuring a sharded cluster* recipe in Chapter 5, *High Scalability with Sharding*, on how to create a sharded cluster.

Additionally, we will also need a previously generated backup from a sharded cluster; you can refer to the *Creating a backup of a sharded cluster* recipe in Chapter 6, *Managing MogoDB Backups*.

How to do it...

1. Shut down the mongos server.
2. Restore the shards one by one:

    ```
    mongorestore -h 192.168.200.200 -p 27027 --drop --dir /backups/shard1bkp/
    ```

3. Shut down the shards.
4. Restore the config server:

   ```
   mongorestore -h 192.168.200.200 -p 27019 --drop --dir /backups/configbkp/
   ```

5. Start the shards and the mongos servers.

How it works...

We begin by initializing the shard cluster, wherein first we ensure that the CSRS is created and initialized. Next, we start the shard servers and the mongos instances. Once the cluster is initialized, we shut down the mongos server to ensure no data is accidentally written to the cluster. We then restore data on each shard, on one instance as shown in step 2.

Next, in step 3, we stop the MongoDB shards, and in step 4, we restore the config server's data. Finally, once the data is restored, we start the shards and mongos instances. Once the entire cluster is up and running, we can connect to the mongos instance and run the `db.printShardingStatus()` command to confirm the health of the cluster.

> Even the best backup strategies fail until data recovery is tested. In the next chapter, we will look at a recipe called *Monitoring MongoDB backups*, in which we will be looking at automated mechanisms to test backups and their restoration.

8
Monitoring MongoDB

The following recipes are included in this chapter:

- Monitoring MongoDB performance with mongostat
- Checking replication lag of nodes in a replica set
- Monitoring and killing long running operations on MongoDB
- Checking disk I/O usage
- Collecting MongoDB metrics using Diamond and Graphite

Introduction

Monitoring is perhaps one of the most crucial components of any production system. Keeping a close watch on the important metrics and signals emitted by a system can help gain wonderful insights into the system's usage and behavior. It can help you debug issues, identify and optimize bottlenecks, and avoid catastrophic failures. Thankfully, MongoDB comes bundled with useful tools and commands that help us monitor its health and take appropriate measures to ensure its optimal utilization. In this chapter, we will look at various tools such as `mongostat` and `mongotop`, work with database commands that give extremely useful metrics, monitor operating system subsystems, and monitor backups.

Let's get started!

Monitoring MongoDB performance with mongostat

In this recipe, we will take a look at the `mongostat` utility, which is bundled with standard MongoDB binary distributions. This tool gives good insights into MongoDB utilization and is also capable of being used programmatically.

Getting ready

For this recipe, at a minimum, you need a single-node MongoDB setup.

How to do it...

1. Connect to you mongod instance and run a bunch of inserts, updates, and deletes:

   ```
   use mydb

   for(var x=0; x<20000; x++){
     db.mycol.insert({age:(Math.round(Math.random()*100)%20)});
     db.mycol.findAndModify({query: {age:
   (Math.round(Math.random()*100)%20)}, update:{$inc: {age: 2}}});
     db.mycol.remove({age:(Math.round(Math.random()*100)%20)});
   }
   ```

2. In a separate Terminal, execute the `mongostat` command. You should see output similar to this:

insert	query	update	delete	getmore	command	flushes	mapped	vsize	res	faults	qrw	arw	net_in	net_out	conn	time
14	*0	*0	14	0	16|0	0		3.00G	249M	0	0|0	0|1	5.43k	29.7k	2	Oct 9 13:43:50.609
50	*0	*0	49	0	51|0	0		3.00G	248M	0	0|0	0|0	18.7k	37.0k	2	Oct 9 13:43:51.608
623	*0	*0	624	0	626|0	0		3.00G	243M	0	0|0	0|0	235k	152k	2	Oct 9 13:43:52.609
947	*0	*0	947	0	949|0	0		3.00G	243M	0	0|0	0|0	357k	214k	2	Oct 9 13:43:53.609
923	*0	*0	922	0	924|0	0		3.00G	235M	0	0|0	0|0	347k	211k	2	Oct 9 13:43:54.609
893	*0	*0	893	0	897|0	0		3.00G	232M	0	0|0	0|0	336k	205k	2	Oct 9 13:43:55.610
862	*0	*0	863	0	864|0	0		3.00G	232M	0	0|0	0|0	325k	199k	2	Oct 9 13:43:56.609
835	*0	*0	834	0	836|0	0		3.00G	232M	0	0|0	0|0	314k	193k	2	Oct 9 13:43:57.609
802	*0	*0	802	0	804|0	0		3.00G	232M	0	0|0	0|0	302k	186k	2	Oct 9 13:43:58.609
787	*0	*0	787	0	790|0	0		3.00G	232M	0	0|0	0|0	296k	184k	2	Oct 9 13:43:59.609

3. Execute mongostat to only give the insert rate and count:

   ```
   mongostat -o
   'host,metrics.document.inserted.rate()=insert_rate,metrics.document
   .inserted=inserted_count'
   ```

4. You should see output similar to this:

   ```
                    host  insert_rate  inserted_count
   localhost:27017             0          162630
   localhost:27017           918          163547
   localhost:27017          2738          166287
   localhost:27017          2745          169031
   localhost:27017          2652          171683
   localhost:27017           945          172630
   localhost:27017             0          172630
   localhost:27017             0          172630
   ```

5. Execute mongostat to run once and give output in JSON:

   ```
   mongostat -n 1 --json | python -m json.tool
   ```

6. You should see output similar to this:

   ```
   {
           "localhost:27017": {
           "arw": "0|0",
           "command": "2|0",
           "conn": "2",
           "delete": "*0",
           "faults": "0",
           "flushes": "0",
           "getmore": "0",
           "insert": "*0",
           "mapped": "",
           "net_in": "158b",
           "net_out": "27.1k",
           "qrw": "0|0",
           "query": "*0",
           "res": "218M",
           "time": "13:29:41",
           "update": "*0",
           "vsize": "2.99G"
       }
   }
   ```

How it works...

We begin by connecting to the MongoDB instance using the mongo shell. In order to simulate operations, we execute a JavaScript code snippet that will insert a 100,000 documents in the database. This should give us a few seconds to switch to another terminal window and see `mongostat` in action.

In step 2, we execute the `mongostat` utility with no command-line parameters. The default output is pretty detailed and will execute indefinitely until you hit *Ctrl + C*. In the sample output, each column represents a particular metric, explained as follows:

Metric	Description
`insert`, `query`, `update`, and `delete`	This denotes the rate of query type per second
`getmore`	This is the rate of cursor batch fetches per second
`command`	This denotes the number of commands per second
`flushes`	For MMAPv1, this represents the number of fsyncs per second, whereas for WiredTiger Engine, it represents the rate of checkpoints per polling interval
`mapped`	This is the size of total data mapped for the MMAPv1 storage engine
`vsize` and `res`	This is the virtual and resident memory size of the mongod/mongos process
`faults`	For MMAPv1 only, this represents the number of page faults per second
`qr` and `qw`	This denotes the queue length of active clients waiting for reads and writes respectively
`ar` and `aw`	This is the current number of active clients performing read and write operations

The `mongostat` utility also allows customization of the fields in its output. In step 3, we execute `mongostat` with the -o option along with the list of fields that need to be displayed in the output. Note that we are adding the `rate()` function at the end of the `insert` metrics. This function shows the rate per second of the given metric. Additionally, `mongostat` also provides a `diff()` function that can show the difference between the current and the previous values of the given metric.

> **TIP**
> When using the -o or -O option, make sure you do not have spaces between the comma separated fields otherwise you will end up in a debugging rabbit hole.

Lastly, in step 4, we take an overly simplistic example to show how `mongostat` can also generate output in JSON format. It can be an extremely handy tool to fetch metrics in a serialized format and parse it to a script.

See also

- For more comprehensive list of mongostat's parameters, refer to the official manual at https://docs.mongodb.com/manual/reference/program/mongostat

Checking replication lag of nodes in a replica set

The most ideal state for a replica set is when all nodes within the cluster are in sync. In this recipe, we will look at how to check the replication lag of nodes in a replica set.

Getting ready

We will need at least a multinode replica set cluster. You can refer to the *Adding a node in a replica set* recipe in `Chapter 4`, *High Availability with Replication,* for more details.

How to do it...

1. Ensure all nodes are up and connect to the primary node of the replica set using mongo shell.
2. Fetch the current replication information:

   ```
   rs.printReplicationInfo()
   ```

3. You should see output similar to this:

   ```
   configured oplog size: 1578.62548828125MB
   log length start to end: 142363secs (39.55hrs)
   oplog first event time: Sun Oct 08 2017 18:54:12 GMT+0530 (IST)
   oplog last event time: Tue Oct 10 2017 10:26:55 GMT+0530 (IST)
   now: Tue Oct 10 2017 10:26:59 GMT+0530 (IST)
   ```

4. Check the current replication information:

   ```
   rs.printSlaveReplicationInfo()
   ```

5. You should see output similar to this:

   ```
   source: 192.168.200.200:27018
   syncedTo: Tue Oct 10 2017 10:28:35 GMT+0530 (IST)
       0 secs (0 hrs) behind the primary
   source: 192.168.200.200:27019
       syncedTo: Tue Oct 10 2017 10:28:35 GMT+0530 (IST)
       0 secs (0 hrs) behind the primary
   ```

6. Shut down one of the secondary replica set nodes, and execute the following query on the primary node:

   ```
   use mydb

   for(var x=0; x<100000; x++){
     db.mycol.insert({age:(Math.round(Math.random()*100)%20)});
     db.mycol.findAndModify({query: {age:
   (Math.round(Math.random()*100)%20)}, update:{$inc: {age: 2}}});
     db.mycol.remove({age:(Math.round(Math.random()*100)%20)});
   }
   ```

7. Start the replica set secondary, and immediately check the slave replication information:

   ```
   rs.printSlaveReplicationInfo()
   ```

8. You should see output similar to this:

   ```
   source: 192.168.200.200:27018
       syncedTo: Tue Oct 10 2017 10:30:11 GMT+0530 (IST)
       0 secs (0 hrs) behind the primary
   source: 192.168.200.200:27019
       syncedTo: Tue Oct 10 2017 10:29:45 GMT+0530 (IST)
       26 secs (0.01 hrs) behind the primary
   ```

How it works...

We begin by bringing up a multinode replica set cluster. In step 2, while connected to the primary instance of the replica set, we execute the `rs.printReplicationInfo()` command. This command prints out the details pertaining to oplog. Oplogs, or operation logs, are database operations performed on the primary node of a replica set. They are stored in a capped collection and are replayed on the secondary nodes within a replica set. This is the core mechanism of how nodes within a replica set are synchronized. Coming back to the `rs.printReplicationInfo()` command's output, we can see the details of the current size of the oplog when it started and the timestamps of the first and last events. This can be a good reference point to know the current state of replication in the cluster.

In step 3, we execute the `rs.printSlaveReplicationInfo()` command, which prints the point in time status of the last event in the respective replica set nodes. Each oplog entry has a timestamp associated with it; hence, by knowing the last event's timestamp, MongoDB can determine the lag between the secondary and the primary nodes of the replica set. The `rs.printSlaveReplicationInfo()` command does exactly this. If you type `rs.printSlaveReplicationInfo` (without the parenthesis), you can view the source of this command, and it will help you understand how this command simply iterates through each member of the replica set and calculates the difference between the timestamps. In our sample output, you can see that we have two secondary nodes in the replica set, and both are in sync with the primary.

In step 4, we run a simple JavaScript snippet that will help us simulate some traffic, and at the same time, we ensure that one of the replica set secondary nodes is turned off. As this snippet takes a few seconds to execute, we attempt to bring this secondary node online with the aim to create an artificial lag between it and the primary node. Immediately, switch to the primary node's mongo shell and execute the `rs.printSlaveReplicationInfo()` command. As shown in the sample output, the secondary node is now catching up to the primary, and hence, it is lagging behind by 26 seconds.

In a production environment, replication lags are pretty common. Factors such as network congestion, disk I/O limitations, memory limitations, and so on can be some of the causes for a node to start lagging. It is one of the most important metrics of a replica set that should always be monitored.

There is a very good Nagios plugin project that can be a good starting point to set up a monitor for a replica log. Even if you are not using the Nagios monitoring system, this plugin can still be used as a standalone monitoring script. Source code is available at: https://github.com/mzupan/nagios-plugin-mongodb.

Monitoring and killing long running operations on MongoDB

In this recipe, we will look at how to find and monitor operations on MongoDB. This can help us keep an eye on any anomalous behavior or catch suboptimal queries.

Getting ready

All you need is a single-node MongoDB instance. Additionally, in order to simulate a busy production system, you may need to add a collection with a couple of million documents. If you are lazy like me, simply run the following:

```
for x in $(seq 30); do mongoimport -h 192.168.200.200 --type csv --headerline -d mydb -c mycol chapter_2_mock_data.csv;done
```

How to do it...

1. In one Terminal window, connect to the mongod instance using mongo shell and run a `find()` query for a string that does not exist in the database:

   ```
   db.people.find({name: 'Foobar'})
   ```

2. In another Terminal window, connect to the mongod instance using mongo shell and run `db.currentOp()`:

   ```
   use mydb
   
   db.currentOp()
   ```

3. You should see output similar to this:

   ```
   {
       "inprog" : [
           {
               "desc" : "conn11",
               "threadId" : "139774219482880",
               "connectionId" : 11,
               "client" : "127.0.0.1:33822",
               "appName" : "MongoDB Shell",
               "clientMetadata" : {
                   "application" : {
                       "name" : "MongoDB Shell"
                   },
                   "driver" : {
                       "name" : "MongoDB Internal Client",
                       "version" : "3.4.6"
                   },
                   "os" : {
                       "type" : "Linux",
                       "name" : "Ubuntu",
                       "architecture" : "x86_64",
                       "version" : "14.04"
                   }
               },
               "active" : true,
               "opid" : 348294,
               "secs_running" : 0,
               "microsecs_running" : NumberLong(543337),
               "op" : "query",
               "ns" : "mydb.people",
               "query" : {
   ```

```
                            "find" : "people",
                            "filter" : {
                                "name" : "Fubar"
                            }
                        },
                        "planSummary" : "COLLSCAN",
                        "numYields" : 7447,
                        "locks" : {
                            "Global" : "r",
                            "MMAPV1Journal" : "r",
                            "Database" : "r",
                            "Collection" : "R"
                        },
                        "waitingForLock" : false,
                        "lockStats" : {
                            "Global" : {
                                "acquireCount" : {
                                    "r" : NumberLong(14896)
                                }
                            },
                            "MMAPV1Journal" : {
                                "acquireCount" : {
                                    "r" : NumberLong(7448)
                                }
                            },
                            "Database" : {
                                "acquireCount" : {
                                    "r" : NumberLong(7448)
                                }
                            },
                            "Collection" : {
                                "acquireCount" : {
                                    "R" : NumberLong(7448)
                                }
                            }
                        }
                    },
        <-- output truncated -->
```

How it works...

In step 1, assuming we have a good number of records, we run a query for a document that does not exist. Hoping this query should run for a couple of seconds, in step 2, we open a second Terminal window and execute the db.currentOp() command. If you are unsuccessful on the first attempt, increase your dataset and try again.

The db.currentOp() command gives out a list of all running operations on the database. These can be server-initiated operations as well as client-run operations. Each operation comes with its own operation ID, which is represented as the opid key. This is a unique integer that can be used with the db.killOp() command if you wish to kill the operation.

There are a lot of variations to the command. For example, if you want to find all update operations for a particular database that are taking more than one second to execute, you can run the following command:

```
db.currentOp({
    "active" : true,
    "secs_running" : { "$gt" : 1 },
    "op": "update",
    "ns": /^mydb\./
    })
```

See also

- For more information about the flags used in db.currentOp(), refer to this manual: https://docs.mongodb.com/manual/reference/method/db.currentOp

Checking disk I/O usage

As explained in Chapter 2, *Understanding and Managing Indexes*, MongoDB's performance is greatly dependent on the system's available memory and disk type. In this recipe, we will look at a few tools and MongoDB commands that can help us identify disk I/O utilization.

Getting ready

You need a single-node MongoDB instance.

Monitoring MongoDB

How to do it...

1. In a mongo shell, execute the `db.serverStatus()` command:

   ```
   db.serverStatus()
   ```

2. You should see output similar to this:

   ```
   {
       "host" : "vagrant-ubuntu-trusty-64",
       "version" : "3.4.6",
       "process" : "mongod",
       "pid" : NumberLong(20657),
       "uptime" : 5626,
       "uptimeMillis" : NumberLong(5625427),
       "uptimeEstimate" : NumberLong(5625),
       "localTime" : ISODate("2017-10-10T10:02:49.306Z"),
       "asserts" : {
           "regular" : 0,
           "warning" : 0,
           "msg" : 0,
           "user" : 0,
           "rollovers" : 0
       },
       "backgroundFlushing" : {
           "flushes" : 93,
           "total_ms" : 457,
           "average_ms" : 4.913978494623656,
           "last_ms" : 4,
           "last_finished" : ISODate("2017-10-10T10:02:04.054Z")
       },
       "connections" : {
           "current" : 2,
           "available" : 51198,
           "totalCreated" : 41
       },
       <-- output truncated -->
   ```

How it works...

The `db.serverStatus()` command gives an exhaustive list of metrics, each having its own merit. However, for this exercise, we will only concentrate on the ones that provide insights into the server's disk I/O:

- `extra_info.page_faults`: This is a counter that shows the total number of page faults in the system. If you see a sporadic increase in the number of page faults, then chances are that your system's memory is not sufficient to hold the entire working and is falling back to disk reads.
- `wiredTiger.cache.bytes currently in the cache`: This value indicates the current utilization of WiredTiger's in-memory cache. Ideally, it should never exceed the maximum value of the cache size.
- `wiredTiger.cache.pages read into cache` and `wiredTiger.cache.pages written from cache`: These two metrics indicate the pages read and written to and from cache, respectively. A high fluctuation in this metric indicates higher utilization of disk I/O. It can be a good indicator of whether to consider optimizing the working set and/or server resources.

In addition to MongoDB's internal metrics, it is extremely important to monitor the operating system's disk I/O metrics. Tools such as iostat should give a detailed view of the current disk utilization and help you identify bottlenecks.

For example, to view the disk I/O of /dev/sda at an interval of 2 seconds, run the following command:

```
iostat -x sda 2
```

This should give an output similar to this:

```
avg-cpu:  %user   %nice %system %iowait  %steal   %idle
           0.52    0.00    0.00    0.00    0.00   99.48

Device:         rrqm/s   wrqm/s     r/s     w/s    rkB/s    wkB/s avgrq-sz avgqu-sz   await r_await w_await  svctm  %util
sda               0.00     0.00    0.00    0.00     0.00     0.00     0.00     0.00    0.00    0.00    0.00   0.00   0.00
```

Collecting MongoDB metrics using Diamond and Graphite

In this recipe, we will look at how to fetch metrics using Diamond metrics collector and send it to Graphite, a tool to store and view time series data.

Getting ready

You need a single-node MongoDB instance.

How to do it...

1. Assuming you are using a Ubuntu/Debian system, install Diamond:

   ```
   sudo apt install python-pip
   ```

   ```
   sudo pip install diamond
   ```

2. Create required directories and the Diamond configuration file:

   ```
   mkdir /etc/diamond
   ```

   ```
   mkdir /var/log/diamond
   ```

3. Download the Graphite docker image, and start the container:

   ```
   docker run -d\
   --name graphite\
   --restart=always\
   -p 80:80\
   -p 2003-2004:2003-2004\
   -p 2023-2024:2023-2024\
   -p 8125:8125/udp\
   -p 8126:8126\
   graphiteapp/graphite-statsd
   ```

4. Start the Diamond collector:

   ```
   /usr/local/bin/diamond -f
   ```

5. Check the Diamond log file (`/var/log/diamond/diamond.log`) and ensure metrics are being collected.
6. Check the Graphite web UI. You should see your metrics as shown in the following sample:

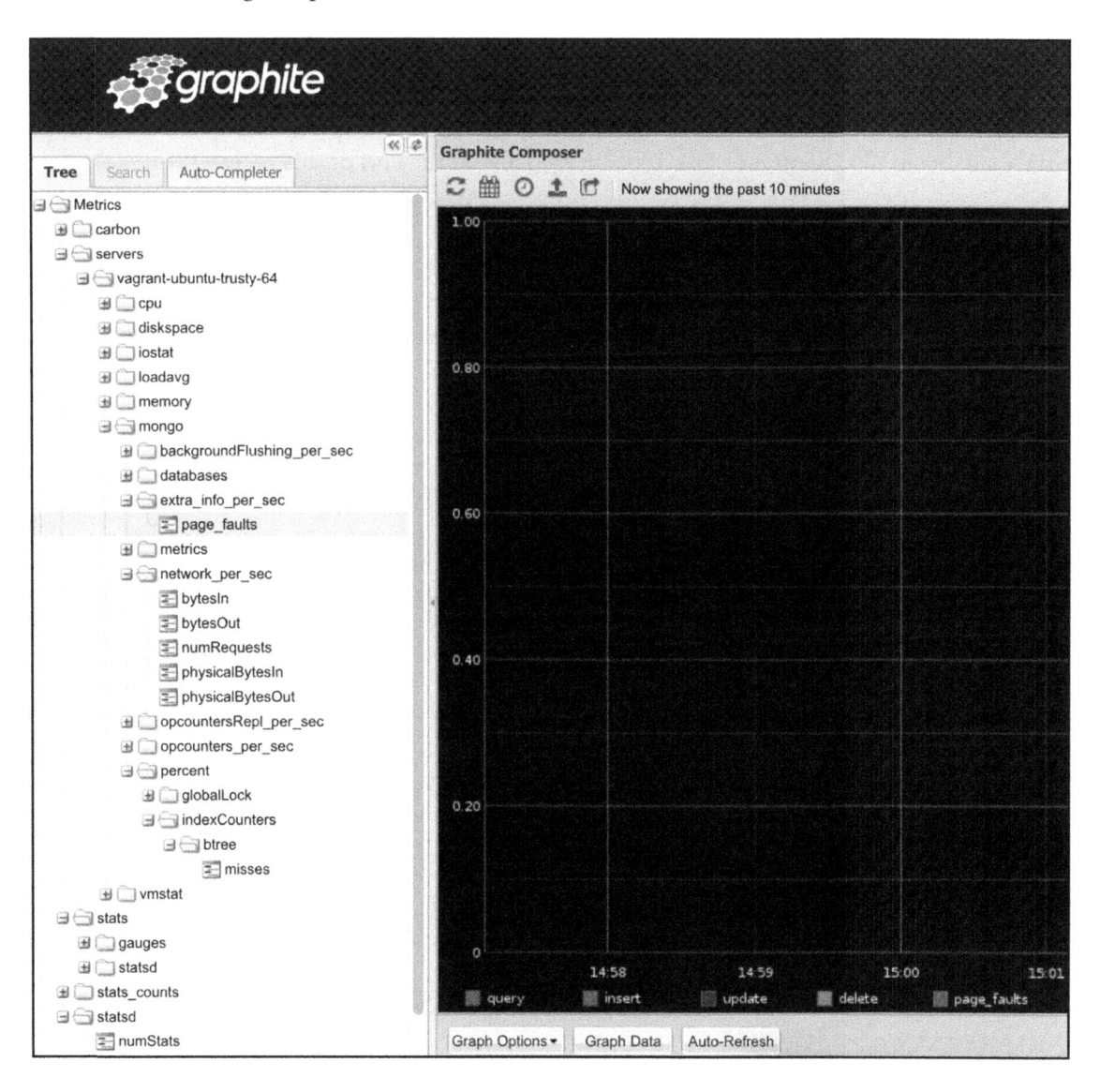

How it works...

Diamond is an open source tool that was built to collect metrics and transfer them to handlers. Graphite is another open source suite that can be used to collect time series data and plot graphs against it.

In step 1, we download the Diamond application using the Python `pip` installer. Once downloaded, we copy the `diamond.conf` file supplied with this book to the `/etc/diamond` directory. If you are industrious, you can copy the sample configuration file available in the Diamond's `git` repository listed at the end of this recipe.

Next in step 3, we fetch the Graphite Docker image and start a container that initiates the Graphite UI as well as its carbon metrics collector.

In step 4, we start the Diamond server in the foreground, and in another Terminal window, we monitor the Diamond collector's log file to ensure it is able to emit metrics to the Graphite server. If all goes well, you should see the Graphite UI on your server's TCP port `80` with a screen similar to the preceding screenshot.

See also

- For more information on the tools used, refer to these links: for Diamond: `https://diamond.readthedocs.io` and for Graphite: `http://graphite.readthedocs.io</a>`

9
Authentication and Security in MongoDB

In this chapter, we will cover the following recipes:

- Setting up authentication in MongoDB and creating a superuser account
- Creating normal users and assigning built-in roles
- Creating and assigning custom roles
- Restoring access if you are locked out
- Using key files to authenticate servers in a replica set

Introduction

Databases are notoriously overlooked when it comes to security. Many a times, engineers assume that, because their application abstracts the underlying database, the actual database systems are untouchable to the outside world. However, if you were to think of the first principles, you have to make sure your database systems are completely locked down, not only to the outside world but also within your infrastructure. Every application, user, or server that needs to communicate with the database system should do so through a well-established **access control list** (**ACL**) mechanism. Thankfully, MongoDB provides a great deal of features that can help facilitate robust authentication and authorization models. In this chapter, we will look at how to implement various authentication and authorization rules to ensure that your production systems are secure. We will begin by creating a superuser and enabling authentication in MongoDB. Lastly, we will look at various role-based access models, creating custom roles, and managing passwords.

Setting up authentication in MongoDB and creating a superuser account

In this recipe, we will look at how to create a superuser account in MongoDB and force MongoDB to use authentication.

Getting ready

You need a standard MongoDB installation.

How to do it...

1. Assuming you already have mongod running, connect to the mongod instance using the mongo shell and switch to the `admin` database:

    ```
    use admin
    ```

2. Create a superuser account:

    ```
    db.createUser(
      {
        user: "superadmin",
        pwd: "supasecret",
        roles: [{role: "root", db: "admin"}]
      }
    )
    ```

3. You should see an output similar to this:

    ```
    Successfully added user: {
    "user" : "superadmin",
            "roles" : [
                    {
                            "role" : "root",
                            "db" : "admin"
                    }
            ]
    }
    ```

4. Restart the mongod instance with `auth` enabled:

   ```
   mongod --dbpath /data/db --auth
   ```

5. Connect to the mongod instance and attempt any regular operation:

   ```
   show dbs
   ```

6. You should see an output similar to this:

   ```
   2017-10-12T11:21:09.966+0000 E QUERY [thread1] Error: listDatabases failed:{
           "ok" : 0,
           "errmsg" : "not authorized on admin to execute command { listDatabases: 1.0 }",
           "code" : 13,
           "codeName" : "Unauthorized"
   }
   ```

7. Authenticate the mongod instance:

   ```
   use admin

   db.auth('superadmin', 'supasecret')
   ```

8. Try any database operation again:

   ```
   show dbs

   db.mydb.foo.insert({a:1})
   ```

How it works...

We begin by connecting to a standard mongod instance and switch to the `admin` database. All users and roles are stored in the `system.users` and `system.roles` collections, respectively. These collections are stored in the `admin` database.

> In a sharded cluster, the `admin` database is located on the config server.

In step 2, we use the `db.addUser()` command to add a user with the options for its username, password, and the role. The `roles` field is an array that can be used to grant multiple roles, specific to a particular operation on a particular namespace. In our case, we create a user called `superuser` with password as `supasecret`. Additionally, we grant this user the role of root to the `admin` database. The role of root is pretty much the highest level role and it allows almost all operations to the system. By granting this role in the `admin` database, we ensure that this user has the administrative privileges to manage all users, databases, and clusters as well as restoration and backup privileges. We will look into the details of the roles in the next recipe.

Next, in step 4, we restart the mongod instance, but this time with an additional flag of `--auth`. This flag forces mongod to prevent any attempted operation until the client (user) is authenticated. We can see in step 4 that even the simplest of operations such as `show dbs` will not work until the user is authenticated.

In order to authenticate, we use the `db.auth()` command after selecting the `admin` database. This command accepts a username and password as its parameters and returns 1 if successful. Once a user is authenticated, you can do pretty much anything with this new superuser!

Creating normal users and assigning built-in roles

In this recipe, we will look at how to use built-in roles provided by MongoDB and assign them to users.

Getting ready

You should have a MongoDB instance with authentication enabled and an administrator account created. Refer to the first recipe of this chapter for more details.

How to do it...

1. Connect to the mongod instance using the mongo shell and authenticate as `superadmin`:

   ```
   use admin

   db.auth('superadmin', 'supasecret')
   ```

2. Create a new user and assign it a built-in role:

   ```
   use mydb

   db.createUser(
     {
       user: "mydb_user",
       pwd: "secret",
       roles: [{role: "read", db: "mydb"}]
     }
   )
   ```

3. You should see that an output similar to this:

   ```
   Successfully added user: {
           "user" : "mydb_user",
           "roles" : [
                   {
                           "role" : "read",
                           "db" : "mydb"
                   }
           ]
   }
   ```

4. Connect to the mongod instance and authenticate.

   ```
   use mydb

   db.auth('mydb_user', 'secret')
   ```

5. Execute a `count()` command:

   ```
   db.mockdata.count()
   ```

6. You should see an output similar to this

   ```
   100000
   ```

7. Now try to insert a document

   ```
   db.foo.insert({bar:1})
   ```

8. You should see an output similar to this:

   ```
   WriteResult({
       "writeError" : {
           "code" : 13,
           "errmsg" : "not authorized on mydb to execute command { insert: \"foo\", documents: [ { _id: ObjectId('59df6b03a535375680f37358'), bar: 1.0 } ], ordered: true }"
       }
   })
   ```

How it works...

We begin by connecting to the mongod instance, switching to the `admin` database, and authenticating with the `superadmin` account. This is the same account we created in the first recipe of this chapter; it has root privileges. Next, in step 2, we switch to the `mydb` database and use the `db.createUser()` command to add a user. By doing so, we ensure that the user created is scoped to the `mydb` database. In the `roles` field, we add the built-in role `read`, limited to the `mydb` database. The `read` role is a MongoDB built-in role that grants access to a certain set of commands to any non-system database mentioned in the `db` field. MongoDB built-in roles are further classified into database-specific user roles, database-specific admin roles, backup and restoration roles, cluster management roles, and so on.

The following list of roles is available for database-specific user roles:

Role name	Commands available in the role
read	- `collStats` - `dbHash</kbd>` - `dbStats` - `find` - `killCursors` - `listIndexes` - `listCollections`

| readWrite | • collStats
• convertToCapped
• createCollection
• dbHash
• dbStats
• dropCollection
• createIndex
• dropIndex
• find
• insert
• killCursors
• listIndexes
• listCollections
• remove
• renameCollectionSameDB
• update |
|---|---|

In step 4, we disconnect from the mongo shell and reconnect back. We switch to the `mydb` database and authenticate using the newly created user, `mydb_user`. Once authenticated, we can run only specific queries (as listed in the preceding table) and any other operations field. This can be seen in the sample output, where a `find()` command works perfectly fine but an `insert()` query is denied.

If you wish to see the users and corresponding roles of a database, you can run the `db.getUsers()` command. The output would be an array of users associated with the database and their roles:

```
[
  {
    "_id" : "mydb.foo",
    "user" : "foo",
    "db" : "mydb",
    "roles" : [ ]
  },
  {
    "_id" : "mydb.mydb_user",
    "user" : "mydb_user",
    "db" : "mydb",
    "roles" : [
      {
        "role" : "read",
        "db" : "mydb"
      }
```

```
      ]
    }
]
```

See also...

For more information about other types of built-in roles, go through the following documentation: https://docs.mongodb.com/manual/reference/built-in-roles.

Creating and assigning custom roles

In this recipe, we will look at how to create a custom role and assign it to users. We will also have a quick look at how to add roles to and revoke roles from a user.

Getting ready

You will need a standard MongoDB installation. Additionally, we will continue from the previous recipe, where we had created a database user and assigned it a built-in role.

How to do it...

1. Connect to the mongod instance using the mongo shell and authenticate as superuser:

    ```
    use admin

    db.auth('superadmin', 'supasecret')
    ```

2. Switch to mydb and create a new role:

    ```
    use mydb

    db.createRole(
      {
        role: "InsertAndReadOnly",
        privileges: [
          {
            actions: [ "find", "insert" ],
    ```

```
                resource: { db: "mydb", collection: "mockdata" }
            }
        ],
        roles: []
    }
)
```

3. Use the `db.getRole()` command to view the newly created role:

   ```
   db.getRole('InsertAndReadOnly' , { showPrivileges: true })
   ```

4. You should see an output similar to this:

   ```
   {
     "role" : "InsertAndReadOnly",
     "db" : "mydb",
     "isBuiltin" : false,
     "roles" : [ ],
     "inheritedRoles" : [ ],
     "privileges" : [
       {
         "resource" : {
           "db" : "mydb",
           "collection" : "mockdata"
         },
         "actions" : [
           "find",
           "insert"
         ]
       }
     ],
     "inheritedPrivileges" : [
       {
         "resource" : {
           "db" : "mydb",
           "collection" : "mockdata"
         },
         "actions" : [
           "find",
           "insert"
         ]
       }
     ]
   }
   ```

5. Fetch the list of roles assigned to the user `mydb_user`:

   ```
   db.getUser('mydb_user')
   ```

Authentication and Security in MongoDB

6. You should see an output similar to this:

    ```
    {
      "_id" : "mydb.mydb_user",
      "user" : "mydb_user",
      "db" : "mydb",
      "roles" : [
        {
          "role" : "read",
          "db" : "mydb"
        }
      ]
    }
    ```

7. Remove the previously assigned role from `mydb_user`:

    ```
    db.revokeRolesFromUser(
      "mydb_user",
      [
        { role: "read", db: "mydb" }
      ]
    )
    ```

8. If you check the roles for `mydb_user` again, the value should be empty:

    ```
    db.getUser('mydb_user')
    ```

9. You should see the `roles` key is empty:

    ```
    {
      "_id" : "mydb.mydb_user",
      "user" : "mydb_user",
      "db" : "mydb",
      "roles" : [ ]
    }
    ```

10. Assign the newly created role to `mydb_user`:

    ```
    db.grantRolesToUser(
      "mydb_user",
      [
        { role: "InsertAndReadOnly", db: "mydb" }
      ]
    )
    ```

[186]

11. Check the roles for `mydb_user` again:

    ```
    db.getUser('mydb_user')
    ```

12. The role should now show the `InsertAndReadOnly` value:

    ```
    {
      "_id" : "mydb.mydb_user",
      "user" : "mydb_user",
      "db" : "mydb",
      "roles" : [
        {
          "role" : "InsertAndReadOnly",
          "db" : "mydb"
        }
      ]
    }
    ```

13. Test the role by inserting a document and then removing the document:

    ```
    db.mockdata.insert({foo:'bar'})
    ```

14. The preceding command should work with the following output:

    ```
    WriteResult({ "nInserted" : 1 })
    ```

15. Attempt to remove a record:

    ```
    db.mockdata.remove({foo:'bar'})
    ```

16. This command should give you an error message similar to this:

    ```
    WriteResult({
        "writeError" : {
            "code" : 13,
            "errmsg" : "not authorized on mydb to execute command { delete: \"mockdata\", deletes: [ { q: { foo: \"bar\" }, limit: 0.0 } ], ordered: true }"
        }
    })
    ```

How it works...

We begin by authenticating as the superadmin user previously created. In step 2, we switch to the database where we want to create the new role. By using the `db.createRole()` command, we create a new role called `InsertAndReadOnly` in the `mydb` database. Roles are defined as a tuple of actions and resources in which we grant a set of actions as an array of command names against a set of resources. The latter is a document that consists of the database name and the name of the collection. I would also like to point out that roles can inherit from other roles. This can be achieved by adding another key called `roles` in the `db.createRole()` command.

For example:

```
db.createRole(
  {
    role: "InsertAndReadOnly",
    privileges: [
      {
        actions: [ "find", "insert" ],
        resource: { db: "mydb", collection: "mockdata" }
      }
    ],
    roles: [{role: "<role>", db: "&lt;database>"}]
  }
)
```

The preceding command would create a new role with specified privileges as well as inherit the privileges from `<role>` and apply it to `<database>`.

Once the custom role is created, in step 3, we use the `db.getRole()` command to fetch the details of a given role. In step 5, we fetch the details of `mydb_user` by executing the `db.getUser()` command. This command lists the details for the given user, including the roles assigned to it. In our example, this user already has a built-in role, `read`, assigned to `mydb`. Let's change that.

In step 5, we revoke the user's roles by executing the `db.revokeRolesFromUser()` command and specifying the username as well as role(s) that need to be removed. We confirm that the role was revoked by executing `db.getUser('mydb_user')`.

Next, in step 7, we add a role to the user by executing `db.grantRolesToUser()`. This command appends a role to the list of roles for a given user, so you need not worry about overwriting any previously assigned roles.

Lastly, we test the scope of the role by successfully inserting a document in the collection and, at the same time, not being able to remove a document from the collection.

When running database systems, people usually tend to only rely on authentication and forget to limit the scope of a given user's access. Roles can be an extremely useful aspect of authorization. By assigning roles and limiting the scope of a user's access to the databases, production database systems can be made more secure.

Restoring access if you are locked out

In this recipe, we will look at how to restore the password for a super administrator user.

Getting ready

You should have a MongoDB instance with authentication enabled and an administrator account created. Refer to the *Setting up authentication in MongoDB and creating a superuser account* recipe of this chapter.

How to do it...

1. Shut down the mongod instance.
2. Start the mongod instance without the `--auth` parameter:

    ```
    mongod --dbpath /data/db
    ```

3. Switch to the `admin` database:

    ```
    use admin
    ```

4. Find the administrative user:

    ```
    db.system.users.find({'roles.role': "root"})
    ```

5. You should see an output similar to this:

    ```
    {
      "_id" : "admin.superadmin",
      "user" : "superadmin",
      "db" : "admin",
      "credentials" : {
    ```

```
                "SCRAM-SHA-1" : {
                  "iterationCount" : 10000,
                  "salt" : "X3IUy53syah8GEZozwwCPA==",
                  "storedKey" : "nzGTHW7yeKUjGxYWEJNkCkzcQZU=",
                  "serverKey" : "HiUfRvoW4MyiOQvtWk3FbLy4bvg="
                }
            },
            "roles" : [
                {
                  "role" : "root",
                  "db" : "admin"
                }
            ]
        }
```

6. Change the password for the administrative user:

    `db.changeUserPassword("superadmin", "Correct Horse Battery Staple")`

7. Start the mongod instance with the `--auth` parameter:

    `mongod --dbpath /data/db --auth`

8. Test the account:

    `use admin`

    `db.auth("superadmin", "Correct Horse Battery Staple")`

9. The preceding command should give you an output of `1`.

How it works...

This is a fairly straightforward recipe. We begin by shutting down the mongod instance and starting it again without the `--auth` parameter. By doing so, we start the mongod instance without authentication support. Next, in step 3, we switch to the `admin` database and, in step 4, we execute a `find()` query to search for any users who already have the root built-in role assigned to them.

In step 6, we execute the `db.changeUserPassword()` command with the target username and its new password. Once we are done, we can stop and start the mongod instance again, this time with the `--auth` parameter to ensure that authentication is enabled.

On a running system, if you already have an administrative user, you can change any user's password using the `db.changeUserPassword()` command. You do not need to shut down the mongod instance.

> There are other methods to further secure a MongoDB system using firewalls and TLS certificates. We will look at these aspects in the next chapter.

Using key files to authenticate servers in a replica set

For the most part in this chapter, we have discussed how to authenticate and authorize users in MongoDB. However, it is also equally important to ensure that unwanted servers do not get attached to a closed system like replica sets.

In this recipe, we will look at how to achieve inter-server authentication within a MongoDB replica set using key files.

Getting ready

You only need standard MongoDB binaries.

How to do it...

1. We begin by creating a key file using the `openssl` utility:

    ```
    openssl rand -base64 756 > /data/keyfile
    ```

2. Change the file permissions for the key file:

    ```
    chmod 400 /data/keyfile
    ```

3. Start the mongod replica set instances:

    ```
    mongod --dbpath /data/server1/db --replSet MyReplicaSet --port 27017 --keyFile /data/keyfile
    mongod --dbpath /data/server2/db --replSet MyReplicaSet --port 27018 --keyFile /data/keyfile
    ```

Authentication and Security in MongoDB

```
mongod --dbpath /data/server3/db --replSet MyReplicaSet --port
27019 --keyFile /data/keyfile
```

4. Connect to the primary instance:

   ```
   mongo localhost:27017
   ```

5. Initiate the replica set:

   ```
   rs.initiate()
   ```

6. You should see an output similar to this:

   ```
   {
       "info2" : "no configuration specified. Using a default configuration for the set",
       "me" : "vagrant-ubuntu-trusty-64:27017",
       "ok" : 1
   }
   ```

7. Add the remaining replica set instances to the cluster:

   ```
   rs.add('192.168.200.200:27018')
   rs.add('192.168.200.200:27019')
   ```

8. For both of the preceding commands, you should see an output similar to this:

   ```
   { "ok" : 1 }
   ```

9. Create a superuser account:

   ```
   admin = db.getSiblingDB("admin")
   admin.createUser(
     {
       user: "myadmin",
       pwd: "supasecret",
       roles: [ { role: "root", db: "admin" } ]
     }
   )
   ```

[192]

10. Test the account using mongo shell:

    ```
    mongo 192.168.200.200:27017
    use admin
    db.auth('myadmin','supasecret')
    ```

How it works...

A key file is nothing but a regular file that contains a secret. MongoDB allows a key file to contain 6 to 1,024 characters. In our example, we begin by creating a key file using the `openssl` utility; in that, we use the parameters `rand -base64 756` to generate a set of random sequence of 1,024 Base64 characters.

Next, in step 2, we use the `chmod` utility available in Unix to ensure that this newly created key file is not globally readable. The command `chmod 400 <filename>` strips all permissions from the file except read-only to the file owner.

In step 3, we start three instances of MongoDB replica set nodes, each listening on a different port and using a different `--dbpath`. In a more realistic scenario, you would probably be running each instance on a single node. For more information on how to manage replica sets, refer to Chapter 2, *Understanding and Managing Indexes*. In addition to the standard parameters, we use the `--keyFile` parameter to mention that we will be using key-file-based internal authentication. The value of this parameter should be the location of the key file; in our example, it is `/data/keyfile`.

Once the replica set nodes are running, as shown in step 4, we connect to one of the nodes using the mongo shell from the same host as that of the mongod instance. It is extremely important that you connect from the same host; we will cover that in a moment.

In step 4, we initiate the replica set using the `rs.initiate()` command, followed by adding the other two nodes to the replica set using the `rs.add()` command.

Coming back to the point on why we connected using localhost... MongoDB provides a feature known as localhost exception. In it, MongoDB allows you to create the first user and role (optional) when none exist. This is extremely useful when you've enabled authentication mechanism but don't have an initial user to authenticate with. By using the `--keyFile` parameter, we enable not only internal authentication between MongoDB replica set nodes but also client authentication. Hence, if you enable key-file-based authentication, your clients (such as mongo shell) will not work unless they are first authenticated with a valid user.

So in step 7, we create the first superuser using the `db.createUser()` command and assign it the built-in role `root` on the `admin` database. This user should be able to do pretty much any operation on the cluster. We can confirm that the authentication works in step 8, when we attempt to connect to the primary node from an external system and authenticate using the newly created superuser.

There's more...

In this recipe, we saw how to start a new replica set using key files. If you already have a replica set, you can still enable key-file-based authorization but you'll have to carefully sequence your steps, like so:

1. First, add a superuser account as shown previously.
2. Next, create the relevant client accounts that would be used by your applications.
3. Ensure that the applications are using the newly created user accounts.
4. Stop one of the secondaries and start with the parameter `--transitionToAuth` along with `--keyFile`.
5. One by one, restart all secondary nodes with the parameter `--transitionToAuth` along with `--keyFile`.
6. Bring down the primary using `rs.stepDown()`, and once a new primary node is elected, start this instance too, with `--transitionToAuth` along with `--keyFile`.
7. Once all the instances are up, you will have successfully switched to key-file-based authentication. All that remains is to remove the `--transitionToAuth` parameter. This can be done by repeating step 4 to step 6 but without `--transitionToAuth`.

10
Deploying MongoDB in Production

This chapter contains the following recipes:

- Configuring MongoDB for a production deployment</li>
- Upgrading production MongoDB to a newer version
- Setting up and configuring TLS (SSL)
- Restricting network access using firewalls

Introduction

Like all user-friendly applications, MongoDB is extremely easy to set up and run out of the box. The default settings provided by MongoDB may not be optimal for all workloads and this can prove expensive post deployment. Hence, it becomes extremely important to consider the nuances that are involved in setting up a robust MongoDB infrastructure from the get-go.

The aim of this chapter is to highlight the key points that one must consider when deploying and running MongoDB systems in a production environment. We will look at the aspects of configuring MongoDB, operating system settings, and selecting upgrade strategies. Furthermore, we will look at how to encrypt server-to-server communication using TLS certificates. We will also learn how to ensure that selective firewall rules are implemented to restrict access to MongoDB.

Configuring MongoDB for a production deployment

In this recipe, we will look at important factors that should be configured when setting up a MongoDB instance. These include MongoDB as well as operating system parameters.

Getting ready

You will need MongoDB binaries and a Linux operating system.

How to do it...

It is highly recommended by MongoDB that you choose the XFS filesystem over Ext4, especially when using the WiredTiger storage engine. It provides concurrent disk I/O, as well as extends (reduced fragmentation-based allocation of data), which provide significant performance improvement over Ext4. To create an XFS-based volume, simply do the following:

1. Install XFS tools:

   ```
   apt-get install xfsprogs
   ```

2. Create the XFS filesystem:

   ```
   mkfs.xfs /dev/<device-name>
   ```

3. Always choose an SSD over a mechanical disk. Additionally, make sure you measure the disk's performance using either the `mongoperf` utility, as shown in the *Measuring disk I/O performance with mongoperf* recipe in Chapter 3, *Performance Tuning*, or by using the `dd` command, as shown here:

   ```
   dd if=/dev/zero of=/dev/<disk> bs=1M count=1024
   ```

4. The preceding command writes 1 GB of data to the disk and gives you an estimated throughput of the operation. For example:

   ```
   1024+0 records in
   1024+0 records out
   1073741824 bytes (1.1 GB) copied, 1.3648 s, 787 MB/s
   ```

5. Disable **Transparent Huge Pages** (**THP**). THP is a feature of the Linux kernel that allows dynamically sized pages to map memory on systems with a large amounts of memory. As with most databases, including MongoDB, the data allocated in memory is non-contiguous, and hence THP can often cause performance implications. To disable THP, ensure that you add the following two lines to your system's init script (prior to starting MongoDB):

   ```
   echo 'never' > /sys/kernel/mm/transparent_hugepage/enabled
   echo 'never' > /sys/kernel/mm/transparent_hugepage/defrag
   ```

6. Ensure that `ulimit` is set to an optimal number. To check `ulimits`, execute the following command:

   ```
   ulimits -a
   ```

7. The folks at MongoDB recommend the following limits:

   ```
   -f (file size): unlimited
   -t (cpu time): unlimited
   -v (virtual memory): unlimited
   -n (open files): 64000
   -m (memory size): unlimited
   -u (processes/threads): 64000
   ```

8. Use a configuration file and avoid using command-line parameters when running mongod/mongos instances. I would highly recommend using a revision control system such as Git or Mercurial to manage changes in these configuration files.

9. Always shut down MongoDB instances elegantly. You can use either the mongo shell or the `kill` command with SIGINT:

   1. Shutting down mongod using the mongo shell:

      ```
      use admin
      db.shutdownServer()
      ```

   2. Shutting down using the `kill` command:

      ```
      kill -2 <mongod pid>
      ```

10. It is always recommended to not run application servers using a privileged user account such as root. The default MongoDB installation done through a package manager such as `apt` or `yum` creates a user called mongodb in the system. The mongod `init` scripts ensure that the processes are run against this username. However, if you are using custom initialization scripts, please ensure that you always use a low-privileged user.

Upgrading production MongoDB to a newer version

In this recipe, we will look at how to upgrade MongoDB binaries in a replica set. This recipe holds true even for config and shard servers.

Getting ready

We will assume you have a three-node MongoDB replica set.

How to do it...

1. Before even touching a system, go through the release notes carefully. There are serious implications when upgrading binaries that have backward-incompatible changes or variance in operational parameters.
2. Take a full backup of your entire system.
3. If you have installed MongoDB binaries using the operating system's package manager, such as `apt` (Ubuntu) or `yum` (Red Hat/CentOS), the upgrade process might trigger a service restart. Hence, do not install new packages until the service is manually shut down.
4. Log in to one of the secondary nodes in the replica set and shut it down:

    ```
    use admin
    db.shutdownServer()
    ```

5. Once the mongod/mongos instance is shut down, install the upgraded package on the system and start the service.

6. Log in to the mongo shell of the instance and ensure that it has caught up with the primary node using the `rs.status()` command.
7. Repeat steps 3 and 5 for the other secondary node.
8. Finally, log in to the primary node and force it to step down:

    `rs.stepDown()`

9. Check with the `rs.status()` command to ensure that a new primary is elected and all nodes are now syncing with this newly elected primary node. This process may take anywhere from a few seconds to a couple of minutes.
10. Once you have repeated steps 3 and 5 for this node, your cluster should be fully upgraded.

There's more...

When upgrading a sharded cluster, your sequence of steps should be as follows:

1. Log in to the mongos shell and stop the balancer using the `sh.stopBalancer()` command.
2. First upgrade the config server replica set.
3. Upgrade each shard individually.
4. Upgrade the mongos query routers.
5. Finally, connect the mongos shell and start the balancer using the `sh.startBalancer()` command.

Setting up and configuring TLS (SSL)

In this recipe, we will look at how to use X.509 certificates to encrypt traffic sent to MongoDB servers. Although TLS is the actual term used to denote **Transport Layer Security (TLS)**, for legacy naming reasons, it is many a times still referred to as SSL.

Getting ready

You need the standard MongoDB binaries.

How to do it...

1. We will begin by creating our own **Certificate Authority (CA)** to generate self-signed certificates:

   ```
   openssl genrsa -des3 -out ca.key 4096
   openssl req -new -x509 -days 365 -key ca.key -out ca.crt
   ```

2. Create the key for the server:

   ```
   openssl genrsa -out server1.key 2048
   ```

3. Create the **Certificate Signing Request (CSR)** for the server:

   ```
   openssl req -new -subj "/CN=server1.foo.com/O=ACME/C=AU" -key server1.key -out server1.csr
   ```

4. Then create the certificate for the server, signed by the CA:

   ```
   openssl x509 -req -days 365 -in server1.csr -CA ca.crt -CAkey ca.key -set_serial 01 -out server1.crt
   ```

5. Generate the .pem file for the server by concatenating the .key and .crt files into one:

   ```
   cat server1.key server1.crt > server1.pem
   ```

6. Start the mongod instance with the newly created certificate:

   ```
   mongod --dbpath /data/db --sslPEMKeyFile server1.pem --sslMode requireSSL
   ```

7. Connect to the mongo shell using SSL:

   ```
   mongo --ssl --sslCAFile ca.crt server1.foo.com:27017
   ```

How it works...

Although explaining how an SSL/TLS connection works would be out of the scope of this book, I will still try to give a short description of what we are trying to accomplish here. We begin by creating a CA public (ca.crt) and private key (ca.key). The private key will be used to sign any subsequent SSL certificates and can be verified by the CA's public key. In step 1, we use the openssl command to create our own CA key and certificate.

Creating self-signed certificates to be used by servers and clients using this CA is a three-step process. First, as shown in step 2, we generate a private key for our server, where we are going to start the mongod instance. Next, as shown in step 3, we create a CSR, also known as the CSR for this server. As you can see, the `CN` field has to match the hostname of the server; otherwise, your clients fail on hostname validation when attempting to connect to this server. Lastly in step 4, using this CSR, we generate a certificate for the server; it is signed by the private key of our CA.

That's it! You now have a fully functional self-signed SSL certificate to be used on this server. As MongoDB uses a `.pem` file, we concatenate the `.key` and `.crt` files, as shown in step 5. Note that the order of concatenation is important; that is, first the `server1.key` file and then the `server1.crt` file. This way, when the application reads the `.pem` file, it will read the certificate part first and then look for the key used to generate the certificate.

In step 6, we start the mongod instance and provide the path to the pem using the `--sslPEMKeyFile` parameter. Additionally, we have to mention the SSL mode using the `--sslMode` flag. The valid options for this flag are as follows:

- `disabled`: Do not use SSL.
- `allowSSL`: Connections between servers do not use TLS/SSL. For incoming connections, the server accepts both TLS/SSL and non-TLS/non-SSL.
- `preferSSL`: Connections between servers use TLS/SSL. For incoming connections, the server accepts both TLS/SSL and non-TLS/non-SSL.
- `requireSSL`: The server uses and accepts only TLS/SSL encrypted connections.

In our case, we use requireSSL to force all connections to use only SSL mode.

Once the server is started, we can connect to it using the mongo client, while passing it the `--ssl` option. We also have to provide it with the CA file to validate the certificate presented by the server; this is done using the `--sslCAFile` flag.
There you have it! A simple yet robust method to encrypt all communications to your MongoDB service.

It is extremely important that the file permissions and ownership of the key files are kept secure. Assuming you are using `mongodb` as the username, change the ownership of the certificate and keys to user `mongodb` and file permissions to owner read-only, like so:

```
chown mongodb server1.key
chmod 600 server1.key
```

There's more...

In addition to protocol encryption, MongoDB also allows server/client authentication using a certificate. In that, the server/client must present a valid certificate signed by the CA presented with the `--sslCAFile` file.

Restricting network access using firewalls

In this recipe, we will take a quick look at how to use Linux IPTables to add firewall rules that can restrict unwanted access to MongoDB processes.

Getting ready

You need standard MongoDB binaries on a Linux operating system. We are going to use **Uncomplicated Firewall** (**UFW**) tools, which is a handy wrapper built on top of IPTables. We assume that you have a three-node replica set running on the following hosts:

Hostname	IP
server1.foo.com	10.1.1.1
server2.foo.com	10.1.1.2
server3.foo.com	10.1.1.3

How to do it...

1. Most Linux distributions come with a kernel that supports net filters, the network filter API on top of which IPTables is built. We will install UFW, a set of tools that help simplify IPTables configuration:

    ```
    apt-get install ufw
    ```

2. Enable the UFW service:

    ```
    ufw enable
    ```

Deploying MongoDB in Production

3. Add the firewall rules to allow all traffic on port 27017 from known IPs:

   ```
   ufw allow from 10.1.1.1 to any port 27017
   ufw allow from 10.1.1.2 to any port 27017
   ufw allow from 10.1.1.3 to any port 27017
   ```

4. Deny all other incoming requests to port 27017:

   ```
   ufw deny from any to any port 27017
   ```

5. Check the firewall rules:

   ```
   ufw status numbered
   ```

6. You should see an output similar to this:

   ```
   Status: active

        To                         Action      From
        --                         ------      ----
   [ 1] 27017                      ALLOW IN    10.1.1.1
   [ 2] 27017                      ALLOW IN    10.1.1.2
   [ 3] 27017                      ALLOW IN    10.1.1.3
   [ 4] 27017                      DENY IN     Anywhere
   [ 5] 27017 (v6)                 DENY IN     Anywhere (v6)
   ```

How it works...

In the previous chapter, we looked at various methods to implementing authentication and authorization on MongoDB instances. As an avid believer in security by obscurity, I feel application servers should also have access restrictions in place, such that unwanted systems cannot simply connect to the application. In our overly simple example, we looked at how to restrict access to a three-node MongoDB replica set by only allowing access from their IPs to their respective ports (27017) and denying access to anyone else connecting to port 27017.

We began by installing Ubuntu's `ufw` package, in step 1. Next, in step 2, we enabled the UFW service. In step 3, we added three specific rules that allow access from the mentioned IP to any protocol/destination on port 27017. Finally, in step 4, we denied any incoming connection to port 27017.

How does this work? The firewall creates a list of rules, starting from the three allow rules and ending with the deny rule at the bottom. For any incoming connection to port `27017`, if the IP of the client machine matches that in our rules, the connection is let through and any other connection is simply dropped. We can see the sequence of these rules by running the `ufw status numbered` command.

Once this simple firewall rule set is in place, you can further add the IPs of your application servers that will be connecting to the database.

See also

- For more details on how UFW works, refer to `https://help.ubuntu.com/community/UFW`.

Index

A
access control (ACL) 177
access
 restoring 189, 190
Amazon EC2
 storage considerations 77
Amazon Web Services (AWS) 77
arbiter
 working with 97, 101
authentication
 setting up 178, 180

B
background indexes
 creating 45, 48
bsondump tool
 using, to view mongodump output in human readable form 139, 140
built-in roles
 assigning 180, 183
 URL 184

C
Certificate Authority (CA) 15, 200
chunks
 managing 116, 120
 references 121
cluster
 shard, removing 123, 127
collection
 backing up 135, 137
 data, restoring 153
 restoring 150, 152
 slow running collection, searching 77
 subset document, backing up 137, 138
compound indexes
 using 40, 45
config server replica set (CSRS) 144, 159
configuration file
 customizing 23, 24
 URL 25
custom roles
 assigning 184, 189
 creating 184, 189

D
data
 restoring, from collection 153
database
 backing up 135, 137
 data, restoring 153
 restoring 150, 152
db.currentOp()
 reference link 171
db.serverStatus() command
 metrics 173
Diamond
 reference link 176
 used, for collecting MongoDB metrics 174, 176
directories
 separating, per database 20, 23
disk I/O performance
 measuring, with mongoperf 67, 72
disk I/O usage
 checking 171, 173
disks
 configuring, for better I/O 63
 considerations, for selecting storage devices 66
 reading 64
 writing 64
Docker container
 MongoDB, executing 25, 27

E

Elastic Block Storage (EBS)
  about 77
  URL 80
Elastic Compute Cloud (EC2) 77

F

firewalls
  used, for restricting network access 202, 204

G

Graphite
  reference link 176
  used, for collecting MongoDB metrics 174, 176

I

indexes
  creating 29, 35
  managing 35, 39
Input/Output Operations Per Second (IOPS) 66

K

key files
  using, to authenticate servers in replica set 191, 194

L

Linux
  MongoDB, beginning 8
  MongoDB, installing 8

M

macOS
  MongoDB, beginning 10, 12
  MongoDB, installing 10, 12
MongoDB Community Edition
  URL 10
MongoDB storage engine
  MMAPv1 17
  selecting 16
  verdict 17
  WiredTiger 16
MongoDB's official documentation
  URL 76
MongoDB
  beginning, on Linux 8
  beginning, on macOS 10, 12
  configuring, for production deployment 196
  executing, as Docker container 25
  installing, on Linux 8
  installing, on macOS 10, 12
  metrics 164
  metrics, collecting with Diamond 174, 176
  metrics, collecting with Graphite 174, 176
  operations, killing 168, 171
  operations, monitoring 168, 171
  performance, monitoring with mongostat 162, 164
  process, binding to network interface 12
  process, binding to network port 12
  production, upgrading 198
  SSL, enabling 14, 16
  URL 8, 10, 26
MongoDBR17's official documentation
  URL 130
mongodump output
  viewing, in human readable form 139, 140
mongodump tool
  used, for backing up 132, 135
mongoexport tool
  using 143, 144
mongoperf
  disk I/O performance, measuring 67, 72
mongorestore tool
  used, for restoring standalone MongoDB 147, 149
mongos routes queries
  URL 109
mongostat's parameters
  reference link 165
mongostat
  used, for monitoring MongoDB performance 162, 164
monitoring 161
Multi-Version Concurrency Control (MVCC) 17

N

Nagios plugin

reference link 168
NMAPv1 17
non-sharded collection data
  moving 121

O

operations
  slow running operations, searching 72

P

partial index
  creating 54, 58
  reference 58
primary node
  and secondary node, switching between 101
Provisioned IOPS (PIOPS) 78

Q

queries
  slow running queries, searching 72, 77

R

replica set nodes
  creating, with backups 156
  priority, modifying 105, 168
replica sets
  about 83
  configuration, modifying 103, 104
  initializing 84, 90
  node, adding 90, 93
  node, removing 93, 97
  point, creating in time backup 141
  reference link 89
  replication lag of nodes, verifying 165, 168
  servers, authenticating with key files 191, 194
replication lag of nodes
  verifying, in replication set 165

S

secondary node
  and primary node, switching between 101
shard key
  URL 110
shard

removing, from cluster 123, 127
sharded cluster
  backup, creating 144
  configuring 110
  restoring, from backup 159
  setting up 110
sharding
  about 107
  components 107
  config server 108
  mongos query router 108
  shard key, selecting 109
  shard server 109
sparse index
  creating 51, 52, 53
standalone MongoDB
  restoring, with mongorestore tool 147, 149
storage engine
  modifying 18, 20
superuser account
  creating 178, 180

T

time backup
  point, creating of replica sets 141
Transport Layer Security (TLS)
  configuring 199
  enabling, for MongoDB 14, 16
  setting up 199
TTL-based indexes
  creating 49, 50, 51

U

Uncomplicated Firewall (UFW)
  about 202
  URL 204
unique index
  creating 59, 60, 61
users
  creating 180, 183

W

WiredTiger 16, 17
working set
  size, determining 80

X

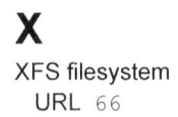

XFS filesystem
 URL 66

Z

zones 127
 about 130

Made in the USA
Coppell, TX
08 September 2021